# SIR EBENEZER HOWARD

## AND

# THE TOWN PLANNING MOVEMENT

EBENEZER HOWARD
*From the painting by Spencer Pryse*

# SIR
# EBENEZER HOWARD

## AND

## THE TOWN PLANNING
## MOVEMENT

Compiled and Written by DUGALD MACFADYEN,
M.A., F.R.HIST.S.

*Omnem novitatem attulit semetipsum afferens*
—IRENÆUS

THE M.I.T. PRESS
Cambridge, Massachusetts

711.4
H84 zm

# CONTENTS

v

# LIST OF ILLUSTRATIONS

Acknowledgments for these illustrations are due and hereby gratefully made to
LADY HOWARD for the Frontispiece : FIRST GARDEN CITY CO. (Letchworth) ;
WELWYN GARDEN CITY CO. ; MANCHESTER CORPORATION (Wythenshawe Com-
mittee) ; GARDEN CITIES AND TOWN PLANNING ASSOCIATION, 3 Gray's Inn Place ;
MR. BARRY PARKER ; MESSRS. BENNETT and BIDWELL ; ST. JOHN RYAN ; A.
CLUTTERBUCK ; JULIAN TAYLOR ; W. FURMSTON ; MRS. BERRY, who have put at
the service of the compiler a larger supply of photographs than have been used.

# FOREWORD

THIS book, being a labour of love, it has been possible to secure the co-operation of those who knew Sir Ebenezer Howard best in both private life and public work. To all whose names appear as contributors, acknowledgments are due for cordial and helpful assistance. Without pooling our resources nothing adequate could have been done.

There are in the book two *motifs*. One is to trace the fortunes of a thoroughly practical and common-sense ideal which had to make its way to recognition, and succeeded in doing so. It is the story of one of the most vital, hopeful, stimulating and successful social movements in the history of England during the last thirty years. The other *motif* is supplied by the development of a personality known to hundreds of people and leaving on all of them a memorable impression. To follow both *motifs* it has been necessary to assemble the facts in separate chapters. Readers interested only in the movement may wish to skip the personal chapters, and readers interested in the man may skip chapters dealing with the movement ; but if so both sets of readers will lose something, for in stark reality the man and the movement were so united that no subtlety of biographical skill could separate their relations and reactions as ideal passes into achievement. This is the permanent interest of the book. Perhaps it is too much to expect that many may find it as interesting to read as it has been to write.

DUGALD MACFADYEN.

BRAMBLE BANK,
  ALINGTON LANE, LETCHWORTH.
    *August*, 1933.

# I

## BEGINNINGS

Man was both lost and saved in a garden.

*Pascal.*

EVERY Biography begins with a birth. Not even the most sceptical will wish to challenge Ebenezer Howard's account of this important event.

' I was born on January 29th, 1850, within sound of Bow Bells in the City of London at 62, Fore Street. My father's name was Ebenezer and he had several confectioners' shops round London. My mother was a farmer's daughter with good common sense, nothing brilliant about her. I had two elder sisters, Elizabeth being still alive, Mrs. Fred Harrison, and Anne Howard, who had a first-class reputation as a typist in the city of London. Fore Street has undergone many changes since 1850 but is still one of those city streets where important-looking warehouses stand cheek by jowl with confectioners and similar shops.'

For the mid-Victorian period the circumstances of Ebenezer's arrival were propitious omens. The son of a man who never had a headache and a farmer's daughter had a hundred per cent chance of a physical constitution which would defy any strain for many years ; and a father doing well in a modest business was able to give him a more useful education than if unnecessary opulence had invited the educational frills which make for extravagant tastes. The London middle-class of the mid-Victorian era, from which both John Ruskin and Robert Browning came, had a mental franchise hardly equalled anywhere else in the country. They had the advantage of all the civilisation there was. They were emancipated from the squire and the parson. Their homes were comparatively secure and they lived by the work of their hands and the enterprise of their brains. Their standard of respectability excluded the vicious habits, the thriftlessness and mental insta-

1

bility of the very rich and the very poor, and tended to make their outlet in life dependent on mental alertness, physical activity and endurance. All this was a part of Ebenezer Howard's inheritance, of which he had a substantial share and made good use.

" At the age of four and a half I was sent to a private school at Sudbury in Suffolk run by two maiden ladies, quiet, sensible women who wrote with quill pens. Here I was well taught, and looking back, I remember I had a special taste for poetry." Quill pens are inimical to quiet, but good sensible women are just the human environment least likely to interfere with the opening of an original, inventive, and adventurous mind—so Ebenezer made headway.

" At nine years of age I went to a school in Cheshunt, Hertfordshire, owned by Mr. Dukes. I well remember there were nine acres to play in, a lovely fishpond and beautiful trees. One of the cedar trees was said to be the finest in Hertfordshire." This early association with Hertfordshire is notable—a latent memory of fair landscapes and wholesome enjoyment would become active when long afterwards the possibility arose of making a first Garden City in one of the choicest counties in England. An eighteenth-century rhyme bears witness to its reputation as a health resort :

> Who buys a house in Hertfordshire
> Pays three years' purchase for the air.

" I was three and a half years at this school before I reached the class I should have entered when starting. I was given simple little pieces of poetry to learn such as :

> Oh come, Mrs. Peacock,
> You must not be proud."

If this recollection is reliable it is an encouragement to slow starters in the educational field. The slow starter is one of the unsolved problems of the educator. He is often the best finisher and frequently makes a better man than the boy who can learn anything in half the time of the rest of the class. But how is a teacher whose pupils are to be examined to find out that he is merely a slow starter and not a duffer ?

" I remember sitting by another boy helping him to do his arithmetic. The master called me out, told me to stand on the form and do a whole page of decimals. Shortly there was a ring

at the front gate. The maid went and who should it be but my
father. The master came up to me and said :

' Ebby dear, your father has come and I have told him what
a good boy you have been.'

" I never did those decimals.

" At twelve years of age I went to Ipswich, Stoke Hall, owned
by Mr. Buck, where I remained till I was fifteen. Then I went
to the office of Messrs. Greaves and Son, Stockbrokers, Warnford
Court, London, where I used to copy letters into a book with a
quill pen. ' He copied out the letters in a big round hand.' Afterwards I was with Mr. C. Elliott, a merchant, for three years, when
I taught myself shorthand. From there I went into the office of
Mr. Edmund Kimber, solicitor, at Winchester Buildings, for a few
months, where I did correspondence." The next step was an
important one.

Dr. Joseph Parker was then at the Poultry Chapel, and with
forceful character and superabundant eloquence was making a deep
impression on the chapel-going folk of London. One of his deacons
was a Mr. Ebenezer Harrison, brother to the Reverend Joshua
Harrison of Park Chapel, Camden Town. His eldest son became
engaged to a sister of Ebenezer Howard. They were the first
couple to be married in the City Temple, Holborn Viaduct, to
which the congregation of the Poultry Chapel migrated with their
minister. They long treasured a Bible which was given them to
commemorate the occasion.

" One Sunday," continues Ebenezer, " I went to Poultry Chapel,
took down Dr. Parker's sermon in shorthand, and sent it to him
with an offer to do this for him every Sunday. Dr. Parker sent
for me to call and asked me to be his private Secretary. I was
with him for about three months until I suppose he got tired of
paying my wages. When sitting down to his correspondence one
day in his study Dr. Parker stopped and said to me :

" ' Mr. Howard, I don't believe in phrenology as some people
do, thinking they can read every bump and pimple on a man's
head, but still in its broad features I think there is something in
it and I should like to feel your head.' I got up, and Dr. Parker
fingered my head.

" ' Mr. Howard, I will say to you what many young men would
have wished me to say to them, but I have been unable to say it.
I think you should have been a preacher. I would rather see you

in a pulpit than any young man I have met for a long time.' "
Not a bad shot for the omniscient Doctor—though he probably
did not recognise the fulfilment of his prophetic utterance when
Ebenezer became a preacher from God's other great word to men
—the book of Nature. A preacher he was of no mean resource
and profundity, though his texts were not always in Dr. Parker's
Bible.

No impressionable young man could come into contact with Dr.
Parker without being profoundly influenced. Small minds recall
his idiosyncrasies, but these were only spots in the sun. He was
a fundamental thinker, which is not the same thing as a funda-
mentalist. His mind had a background. He worked from first
principles, and handled all sorts of subjects in a large way. His
principles were real factors in life to him ; they roused his energies
and when he let go on some subject in which he was interested
the sweep of the current of his thought was like a Niagara torrent.
He had a habit, then unusual, now impossible, of talking in private
in the same rolling, rounded periods which he used in the pulpit. It
can hardly be fanciful to set down something of Ebenezer Howard's
freedom from conventional ways of thinking, his fundamental
originality and constant reference to first principles to his early
contact with a large and forceful human personality which throve
on opposition.

Influences of that sort take a long time to work out. They may
be latent for years, till opportunity or necessity suddenly brings
them into activity. Ebenezer never forgot that he had been Dr.
Parker's Secretary.

# II

## INHERITANCE

> You see there are all those early memories; one cannot get another set:
> one has but these.
>
> *Willa Cather.*

EBENEZER HOWARD had wonderful parents, utterly strenuous and
hard-working, loving, lovable and very human people, generally
liked by all who knew them.[1] I speak of them because they must
have given so much to his making. The Mother, extremely practical, the Father whose eye and nose belonged, I often thought,
to the Viking type, though below the face Nature had managed
only a very very slender and small body, as though there had not
been enough material left over from such a wonderful head and
eye. He used to say, up to when he was seventy or nearly, that
"I have never had a headache in my life." Though work took
him generally from 3 a.m. till quite late he was always most full
of energy, and so vital that his eye was like a flame, but a most
kindly one. The biggest things in his composition were, I think,
an absolute uprightness, perfect truth and sincerity, and a great
humanitarianism—so big that it was really Godlike. Here are
two instances of the latter:

When his two confectioners' businesses in the City, not geographically but financially "went West," he sighed a little but
never demeaned himself by grumbling; he always helped "lame
dogs" by giving them positions in his premises; over this he often
undoubtedly lost in one way and another. I think it was not in
him to refuse help to any.

One day of fog, the driver of a hansom cab drove it, horse and
all, through Uncle Howard's plate-glass window; everything in
window and counter (both full of eatables) was a dead loss; the
man was brought up in court and Uncle had to attend; he was
asked as to his compensation.

[1] Letter from Mrs. E. M. Benn, daughter of Mr. Howard's cousin.

5

"Is the man to pay it?" asked my uncle.

"Yes, the man will have to pay it."

The man had a wife and five little ones and was shaking with fear. With dignity I know well, Uncle explained he was not going forward with this matter.

"How could I act against a poor soul like that?"

Another incident I recall was this : One day a gentleman asked to see him privately—this was unusual and we learned after of an extraordinary meeting between them. The man had come to make confession of *years* when he had consistently eaten meals at Uncle's restaurant without making any payment! Those were not the days of cash desks close to the door, and all who came there to eat were extremely friendly with all who served them (there being a wonderful spirit abroad around those tables because of the man in the bakehouse beneath), yet it sounds incredible. It was true, however, and the man, covered with shame for those past years, had come to make rather big restitution. At that time the money was badly needed, but Uncle's summing up was "Poor soul, it's bad to have anything on the conscience all that time; some folks are built crooked—can hardly help it—but of course I refused his money—it would seem as though I did not forgive, also as we talked I learned he had none too much!" So the man departed with only this :

"Well, friend, I know that sort of thing won't happen again with you." . . .

Uncle never told the man's name ; he was, as my mother often said, "One of Nature's real gentlemen."

"Absent-mindedness" must have been in the family, for Uncle was extremely absent-minded. Though the family forced gold-rimmed spectacles upon him on birthdays he never retained any, their holding was most precarious with him ; one minute on his nose (he was never resting scarcely for an hour together but on Sundays) next he had cried out :

"Vexing, but they're gone! Oh well, perhaps I'll take a walk."

Several of us girls hunted for them, we were so fond of him—and after much perturbation ran them to earth in the coalbox!

"Ah yes, I mended the fire and I suppose shut them in."

I have pleaded : "Uncle, dear, your face should have gold spectacles, not those steel frames; don't lose them again or they say you can't have more."

"Steel frames are quite good enough for me." In his opinion anything was good enough for him.

Uncle was very agile because so slender and light; one day when he was seventy, we girls in the drawing-room with him, he said :

"Would you like to see me vault over that chair ? "

"Oh do, Uncle ! "

"Oh no, don't, you might fall."

"Nonsense," he said. He rose bravely in the air, but his foot brought off the chair top, yet he did not stumble.

"Unfortunate! What will Annie (his daughter) say ? She is out. I think we will take it to the loft and not worry her ! "

He twinkled, yet looked a little worried, so we comforted him.

"Uncle, it is your own furniture, you know ; you can break a chair or two, if you wish ! "

"Right (smiling), so it is ; we will to the loft ! "

Uncle had the fondness of the very young for a good love-story, and if we went upstairs, on a Sunday afternoon, on any errand, we never found our hero and heroine where we had left them— the book had disappeared. In vain we exclaimed to uninterested readers with their own safe heroines :

"I *know* I put it down just here—my book I am speaking of." We hunted in vain. Suddenly an avenging arm swooped down upon Uncle; he was reading from it just where you had left off and was beaming happily; as, indignant, you took it, he pleaded :

"Now just to the end of that page let me go." Sitting on his chair-arm we kept him to that ! Everyone's book went in turn just when you reached the absorbing part where you must bring your characters through . . .

There is obviously no ground for the exaggeration which has described the second Ebenezer Howard as 'born in a slum.' His father was one of a family of nine. That, with the strict English laws of succession, is sufficient to account for the fact that he had to 'do for himself.' Though the pedigree is obscure, his father was probably descended from the Howards of Effingham. The story of the English countryman who goes up to London and is carried along by the growth of London has been well told by Galsworthy in the *Forsyte Saga*. The original Ebenezer Howard of Fore Street might be fitted quite appropriately into that framework. Ebenezer Howard of the Garden City movement had the keen liquid blue eyes, the developed brow, mobile features, the perfect health, clear complexion and the reliable nerve of the English countryside. His voice was a rich baritone, very useful to a speaker. Though it took him a long time to find his *métier*, his reaction to City life was true to type when it came. He knew that the City was no proper environment for the human body.

EBENEZER HOWARD I., FATHER OF THE
FOUNDER OF THE MOVEMENT

# III

## SELF-DISCOVERY

God is in all that liberates and lifts
In all that humbles, sweetens, and controls.

AFTER leaving Dr. Parker's service Ebenezer put in three years with Messrs. Pawle,. Livesey & Fearon, solicitors near Temple Bar. He was then in his nineteenth year, and like many others of whom he had heard he turned westward to the United States in search of a better opening for his energies. Two others, about his own age, went with him—one of them Fred Harrison, a son of Mr. Ebenezer Harrison already mentioned.

" After three years in a solicitor's office where my skill in shorthand was very useful, I went, with two friends, to Nebraska—partly for the benefit, as we anticipated, of the buffaloes," so he said—actually he was following a doctor's prescription for a supposed weakness of his lungs.

The ship in which they sailed took eighteen days to reach New York owing to a burst cylinder.

' At Des Moines, Iowa, we were introduced to some Irish-Canadians, and as they had decided to go to Howard County, Nebraska, we went there too.'

This coincidence in nomenclature did not stand alone.

' They started a little church—I do not mean a building—and took my first name (not however wittingly) as the name of their new congregation.'

So Ebenezer Howard became one of the preaching staff of Ebenezer Church, Howard County, Nebraska. One memory of this period which he recalled afterwards was of the waste of time and labour in farming life due to lack of co-operation.

' After a few months I turned eastward to Chicago and was soon on the staff of Ely and Burnham, stenographers in the Law Courts in that City. Ely had been private Secretary to General

10

Grant and Burnham was even then famous for his discoveries of double stars.

'My stay in Chicago had great influence on my life—giving me a fuller and wider outlook on religious and social questions than I should have gained in England. A professional confrère, Alonzo M. Griffen, of a Quaker family (whom I met again in Detroit years afterwards), helped me greatly in the direction of perfect freedom of thought : and associated with this, a very deep sense of responsibility, and a clear perception that all values, to be rightly estimated, must be assessed mainly by their influence on the spiritual elements in our nature. Thus only can material conditions be widely and permanently improved. We became, as our friends remarked, like brothers.'

One incident in this period stood out in memory as a signpost marking a new direction :

'In 1876 Griffen and I were commissioned by the *Chicago Times* to furnish a verbatim note of an address by Mrs. Cora Richmond. I well remember how deeply we were impressed by the very beautiful invocation which preceded the address.'

'Cora Richmond afterwards became a well-known Christian Science lecturer.[1] Father visited her on several occasions, and on one of these she advised him to give up his endeavours to produce mechanical inventions :

'"I can see no future for you in that line. I see you in the centre of a series of circles working at something which will be of great service to humanity." '

That suggestion coming from a woman whom he regarded as a seer gave him confidence when he came to draw his plan of a Garden City in concentric circles. Among his papers is a manuscript book written by himself of Mrs. Cora Richmond's addresses.

This experience helps to account for the Americanism in Howard's make-up. The special inheritance of the Puritan as we see it philosophically in Emerson, and practically in Ford, is a real conviction that mind triumphs over matter, that a clear idea tends to actualise itself by the inherent force that is in it. The mind of old England works from the concrete to the abstract—the New Englander works from the ideal to the real. Consequently ideals and principles are more a subject of talk with them. They do not

[1] Information from Mrs. Berry.

all achieve themselves and get translated into reality, but they are
not tabooed as ' mere ideals ' as they are with us. ' What ought
to be ' has nearly as much reality as ' what is.' It is something
to ' go for.' It is recognised as a genuine contribution to get an
ideal rightly and well expressed. This tipping of the balance towards the ideal remained in Howard's mind all his life and made
him a stimulant and inspiration rather than an authoritative leader
in the movement he started. It kept him well ahead of his colleagues and associates and sometimes left them panting and breath-
less behind.

The religious outlook so well described by himself, is now known
as Christian Humanism—in which the noblest thoughts of good
men are taken as interpreting the mind of God. It is the most
characteristic contribution which the United States has made to
religious thought, the outcome of Emerson, Lincoln, Lowell, Whit-
man, and many unprofessional religious teachers who have sought
to be true to their own experience, regardless of doctrinal and
ecclesiastical considerations.

The cheerful optimism of an unselfish man, living in a lovable
world, he kept through life. If Chicago did not fill his pockets
with gold it did something better : it fitted him for world
citizenship.

In 1879 Howard returned to England and joined the staff of
Messrs. Gurney & Son, official reporters to the Houses of Parliament. His absence had sharpened his observant eye. He noticed
the haphazard building of London in city and suburbs which had
gone on while he was abroad. He remembered seeing a shop built
in Moorgate Street jutting on the pavement and remarking, " That
building will have to come down." When he returned from
America it was gone.

### § MARRIAGE AND HOME LIFE

It is said that genius is a prolonged adolescence—which appears
to mean that a genius is one who keeps young energies and a fresh
outlook on life long after the time when most men have grown
cynical and discouraged. Marriage is an important factor because
every man is as old as his wife makes him. If she keeps him young
the genius has time to acquire a knowledge of other men and
their ways of thinking, which gives him his opportunity for
putting foundations under the castles in Spain which pleased

his youth. He becomes the Happy Warrior of Wordsworth's poem :

> Who when brought
> Among the tasks of real life has wrought
> Upon the plan that pleased his childish thought.

He refuses to become wise in the commonplace way and to settle down to disillusionment and discontent. If this be anywhere near the truth, Ebenezer Howard had both the opportunity and some of the characteristics of genius—chief among them that he refused to be paralysed by the want of money. He never had much— but he knew there was more money in the world than moneyed people knew what to do with, and his own freedom from the ambition to make money left him free to see its nobler uses. He had the buoyancy of the schoolboys of whom it was written :

> Alas, regardless of expense
> The little urchins play ;
> Of bills to come they have no sense,
> Their sires will have to pay.[1]

In 1879, at the age of 29, Ebenezer Howard married Elizabeth Ann Bills, whose mother had managed an hotel in Nuneaton and attended the same school as George Eliot ; her father was Thomas Bills of Nuneaton. She belonged both to the middle class and the middle English. They had three daughters and one son, and in spite of slender means, their home life was exceptionally happy. ' Neither father nor mother were irritable.[2] They never scolded, never punished, never complained.' The children were generally at Grandfather's in Fore Street when Ebenezer was in America. Their greatest excitement was an annual visit to the gallery at Drury Lane. ' We never had any money but we didn't miss it. Father always had a bright greeting for us and seemed to want us about him, but five minutes afterwards he would be deep in a book and oblivious of our existence. He was always full of schemes which were to make us rich, but he had no luck in that respect. He invented an improvement in the Remington typewriter which was to make a perfect alignment, but when he took it to America Remingtons were not ready to use it. Afterwards they wanted it and wrote asking him to bring it over, but his workshop had meanwhile been burned down and he could not spare the time or the money to do the work over again.

[1] Parody on the *Distant Prospect of Eton College*.     [2] Mrs. Berry.

'His favourite amusement was watching cricket at the Oval. When he could manage it he would spend a whole day there. If he took one of us he would get so absorbed in the game that he forgot we were there.'

Like all optimists he lived in an optimistic universe. 'Even when he met mean people, or occasionally bad people, he didn't know they were "wrong uns," would not believe in their badness, and treated them just as he expected to be treated himself. Mother was the mainspring of our home life. She believed in her husband, shared his belief in Garden Cities and kept him true to his ideal, and she lived to see the land of promise from Mount Pisgah.' The Mrs. Howard Memorial Hall in Letchworth was a public recognition of the part she played in the achievement of Garden City.

'I remember the first meeting at Rectory Road Congregational Church after his book was published.[1] That was the first time I realised that he carried weight on the platform. He held his audience from the first and kept them interested to the end. There was quite an excitement in the congregation about "Mr. Howard's book," as he had never taken any prominent part in Church affairs. The Rev. Fleming Williams, Minister at Rectory Road, backed him up and became a valuable ally—as also did James Branch (L.C.C.) of the Bective Shoe Company.

'John Burns was another of father's friends ; though he approved the aims of the Garden City and admitted the case for it, he refused to be interested in anything outside the boundaries of London. He said "London was big enough for him and required all his energies."

'Horatio Bottomley was at one time a "dictatee" in father's office—that is, father dictated to him from his shorthand notes and it was his part to reproduce the dictation in type. Father worked very long hours. A typical day worked out like this—first in the Courts, then back to his office to dictate, then he waited to correct the typed reports so that they should be "word perfect" for delivery next day. This process of "reading back" to him, on which he insisted, kept him very late at the office.

'When it came to writing *Tomorrow*, the first title of his book, he wrote at our table at home often during meals, dictated to me, and I read it back to him. His office was No. 11 New Court, Carey Street, and all his activities had their centre there.

[1] Mrs. Berry.

'Our homes were various and in different parts of London. At one time in Clapham where we had the Common for playground. Afterwards at 127 Evelyn Road, Rectory Road, which brought us into the range of the Rev. Fleming Williams' influence. This counted for a great deal in our young lives, as we thought Mr. Williams almost superhuman. He looked so fine and was so fond of larking with his own family and ours. We were almost members of his family. Afterwards we had a house at Kyverdale Road, Stoke Newington, and it was from there that *Garden Cities of Tomorrow* was written.'

Mother was the mainspring who kept things going and you see we never had any money are the dominant notes in Mrs. Berry's recollections of this period. The practical common sense of Mrs. Howard—her tact in remembering people—her appreciation of the relative values of helpers in the Garden City movement, impressed others who came to know her in the early stages of the Garden City movement.'

Mrs. Howard made him a wonderful comrade. Through laughing eyes—for she possessed the humour he lacked—she saw all the things his absent-mindedness forgot to do for her ; her little dainty touches of bright fruits and flowers diverted the eye from shabby chairs that must not be renewed, the charming way she presided over a tea-table could hypnotically lead to one eating with vast enjoyment something one never touched otherwise ; from her hands came a daintiness of wearing apparel that could not have been created, had her fingers been less clever, at such trifling cost.

"He is always gentle and even-tempered, never a cross word," she once said to me. "Of course he never knows what he is eating so he does not enjoy it ; still he never grumbles either." She often told this tale :

'It was the first day of our honeymoon ; we were sitting before a very pleasant dinner-table. There was a fowl—we were both hungry. Ben started carving, but to my amazement, he only carved one plate and began eating. I watched with first amazement, then amusement, to see how long this would go on. The plate was nearly empty when he said genially : "This is a delicious dinner, Lizzie dear."

"I expect it is, Ben, but I have not tasted it yet !" Roars of laughter from the family, in which Ben himself joined.'

She passed on without seeing, at least here, the full fruits of his labours and hers ; I can imagine their meeting :

" Well, Ben, so you have not forgotten to come ! "

Being myself a woman I saw the woman's side of the household most clearly,[1] writes one of his cousins : ' My impressions of my relative Ebenezer Howard are almost a sharp contrast. On my first visit to his parents I merely heard of him, he being in America, where many thought his plans (for typewriter additions and improvements) were to the betterment of his position.

" So your son will soon be a rich man, Mrs. Howard." To which his mother replied :

" I will believe in such riches when I see them." She knew him too well to believe he was one of those who would ever own, or keep much money. . . .

' My first connexion with him personally was when, having lost my home, I came to get a position in his office at the Outer Temple. I found cousinship immediately lost in the business man (this term may not seem to apply to him, but in that he worked everlastingly, untiringly and always towards a definite goal, perhaps it is not so out-of-place). He was then one of the, if not *the* most rapid shorthand writer in London ; I greatly admired this in him, for I was on the very humblest rung of the stenographic ladder. If he ever hastily snatched up my book to " see how you progress " I shivered, for always came :

" But it is impossible to write . . . thus . . ."

' He often impressed upon me the great necessity of using every second to improve myself ; when he looked at me, or more often looked over my head, or through me, I felt myself dwindling, smaller and smaller, for day by day I discovered how far removed this man was from daily human life. He never felt ill, or weary, or had a cold like other mortals (at least he gave no sign), always untiring work—work at high speed. Such a man exacted heavily of others ; they also must not flag or be weary. He was amazed that I should shrink, at sixteen, from being sent to speak with a Bank Manager (I who had never entered a Bank at all). Far from excusing me this terror, he saw in the shrinkage good reason for sending me to such places constantly on the principle that " nervousness is too expensive a luxury for one who must be quickly self-supporting." I had the impression that he seldom heard any-

[1] Mrs. Benn.

thing one said ; he was inwardly busy with thought. Later, when I had gone into another office, if he saw me lunching at the place he did, he would then come to my table and spend all lunch time over plans for Garden Cities, and while I ate would, with his finger on his maps, show factory sites, drainage system, etc. etc. Hardly any of it could I properly follow, but the idea of the radiating roads from the centre was, I thought, splendid. One day, looking with his dreamy eyes into the far future, he astonished me by saying :

" But of course we shall have conquered the air and be flying long before that."

' He was not a humorous man at all, I had found, but at this I essayed a gentle laugh ; it brought him to earth with :

" You are intelligent enough to realise that is so ! "

One day his sister came to me asking :

" Will you, in spare time, for love of the cause, type copies of Ben's book *Tomorrow* ? " (as it was first called). " I have not time, and he can't afford to pay for the work."

' Having intimated my willingness, I used, for some time, every spare moment to accomplish this for him and soon handed in the typescript, glad to have done it ; for, in those days he was, so far as I knew, my only relation who had ever written a book, the thing I was always hopelessly longing to do !

' Whenever we met he drew me aside for talk on some very serious topic. Once he began about a bad strike and its misery. *He* was busy, I soon found, among the causes of such misery and their big remedies ; *I* was busy by fireless hearths with desperate men and sad-eyed women who had little ones clinging to them. " Depression in Trade " I now heard of for the first time ; it puzzled me—folks so poor who looked all right ; earnestly I assured him :

" I will prevent myself spending every penny I can and will ask my sister to do the same ! "

' Of course he lifted his hands in horror of this foolishness and I was covered with confusion when he ejaculated (this time looking *at* rather than over or through me) :

" Is it possible you can so misunderstand the situation ! No, my dear child, you must *spend* every pound you possibly can to help this situation." '

It struck me money was to him indeed " nothing, my dear girl, of value in itself—merely a means of exchange." Rapidly he took me back to the days of savage barter, so that when he tried to switch me on to more deep problems I was seeing dark-skinned women with hanging hair and nice little dark velvet-eyed babies ; I got too engrossed where he did not mean me to be ; it was always so.

His extreme absent-mindedness alternately amused and appalled me, when I viewed it as it touched those nearest him ; he himself was aware of it and amused thereat.

" I know I'm absent-minded," he would say. " Once I did a funny thing. I had gone to see Niagara Falls and, as you know, folks can walk a certain distance underneath them. As I walked I began going over all sorts of plans for the future, but presently woke to the fact that there was a lot of shouting, folks were shouting to me to turn back. I had walked much farther than anyone ever was permitted to do and they had been shouting for some time."

I remember the time when he became greatly intrigued with Bellamy's book *Looking Backward*. I think it inspired him.

" You must study it," said he.

" I should love to read it. Is it so wonderful ? "

" Yes, I buy dozens of copies merely to give away." My mind said : " Oh blessed man, I wish you would spare me one," but it never came,—his mind had glided over it already.

§ PERSONALITY

Yours is the praise if mankind
Hath not as yet in its march
Fainted and fallen and died.

*Matthew Arnold.*

It is a reasonable question to ask how a man with Howard's qualities and start in life came to have the undoubted influence he wielded with all sorts of people. One answer to the question is that he had ' personality,' but that only throws the question a stage further back. What was the quality of his personality that made people trust him ? How was it built up ? What elements entered into the make up of his mind and character that made him ordinary enough not to be classed as a ' crank,' and unusual enough to formulate an ideal in a way to capture minds more practical than his own ? Anyone who has tried to allure a company of Englishmen along the shining moon-beam path of the ideal knows how endless are the difficulties—the recurrent questions and objections—the fertility of doubts—the head-shaking over financial problems, the irritating superiority of the arm-chair critic, and the very real perplexity caused by ' cold feet ' of partners in an enterprise who have put their hands to the plough but will insist on looking back to find excuses for ' getting out.'

Howard triumphed over all these obstacles by qualities which he had in excess. He was absolutely convinced that his ideal was right. It filled his mind. He had identified himself with it till it was part of himself. He impressed people as a transparently honest man who ought to be helped to make good. To him it was a sin exciting moral indignation to go on creating slums after a better way of housing the people had become possible. That being so, the negative side of his obsession was that he was impervious to objections.

" *I had the impression that he seldom heard anything one said: he was inwardly busy with thought.*"

When a man has once got his goal clear in his mind everything seems to converge upon it. It would not be true to say that Howard had a ' single track ' mind. His mind was always growing. It remained receptive and open but only for facts, incidents and ideas which bore on his main purpose. His hand and brain work left his inner mind free to work on facts, principles and ideas which he felt to be important. He might even be defended against his own admission that he was absent-minded—for absent-mindedness is frequently the other side of high concentration. The concentration he gave to his ideal explained and was reflected in his absent-mindedness as to present details. If it were possible to define so subtle a factor as the personality which was his main contribution to the movement it might be described as high concentration on an idea which touched every side of human life— intensively exclusive, exclusively intensive.

From the time when Howard became absorbed in his book, *Garden Cities of Tomorrow*, personal history is merged in the dynamic idea. We see him carrying on at his office like a perfect machine, well oiled, with as little friction as possible—turning out his carefully typed reports which kept him in bread and butter—but the inner man which is the real man has moved on into another sphere of interest. With a family dependent on him it was a bold and perilous adventure to sink Ebenezer Howard the stenographer in

Ebenezer Howard the founder of Garden Cities—but having once committed himself to the venture he never looked back. More and more the individual is lost in the movement. Details of his personal life hardly emerge again for twenty years. Just as the personality of St. Paul has to be reconstructed from his treatment of the churches he founded, so Ebenezer Howard's biography becomes merged in the record of how he handled his Garden Cities, and the Town Planning movement which followed them. We can almost watch the development taking shape.

# IV

## GENESIS OF *GARDEN CITIES OF TO-MORROW*

Such men are sensitive to the directions in which progress and destiny lie as an artist is sensitive to beauty.

*Temple Biographies : Introduction.*

On a mentality well stocked, rich in fertile elements and already "working" as gardeners say of the soil, the seed of Bellamy's *Looking Backward* fell and germinated.

'I had already taken part in two very small social experiments unsuccessfully and had twice visited the U.S.A., when in 1898 a friend lent me *Looking Backward*, just published in America but not yet in England. This I read at a sitting, not at all critically, and was fairly carried away by the eloquence and evidently strong convictions of the author. This book graphically pictured the whole American nation organised on co-operative principles—this mighty change coming about with marvellous celerity—the necessary mental and ethical changes having previously occurred with equal rapidity.

'The next morning as I went up to the City from Stamford Hill I realised, as never before, the splendid possibilities of a new civilisation based on service to the community and not on self-interest, at present the dominant motive. Then I determined to take such part as I could, however small it might be, in helping to bring a new civilisation into being. At once I called on Reeves, then in Fleet Street, and suggested that he should publish an English edition of *Looking Backward*. This, on my offering to dispose of at least a hundred copies, he agreed to do. Shortly afterwards, and before writing my book, I joined with a few friends in discussing Bellamy's principles. We gradually discovered some of the author's weak points, the most outstanding being the assumption that such a tremendous change could be effected at once.

' Thus I was led to put forward proposals for testing out Bellamy's principles though on a very much smaller scale—in brief, to build by private enterprise pervaded by public spirit an entirely new town, industrial, residential and agricultural. At this early stage I pictured such a town and all its departments as under the control of a body of Trustees supplying funds but at a low rate of interest.

' Later I began to see other difficulties. The first of these was that of finding men competent and willing to give up other activities in order to manage the agricultural part of the estate. Then the thought flashed into my mind—

" Don't tackle your problem thus. Let your agricultural land to various tenants, securing, as far as possible, the increment of land values for the benefit of the Town's people."

' In another flash came the thought :

" Do the same with your industries."

' Then I felt I was getting on to something like solid ground.

' Shortly after this I wrote the first part of my book, circulating it in typewritten form among a few friends such as Mr. A. L. Leon and Mr. James Branch, members of the London County Council. Mr. Branch gave an address on the scheme at Toynbee Hall, and I spent a good deal of time lecturing about it, chiefly in London. Month after month rolled by and I had done little to bring my proposals before the public, chiefly because I could find no publisher who would take the risk. Then came to the rescue an American friend, Mr. George Dickman, who, like myself, was a great admirer of Mrs. Cora Richmond.

' Mr. Dickman was then Managing Director of the Kodak Company. One evening he said to my late wife who, as he well knew, was a very active helper in our common cause :

" How is Ben getting along with that book ? "

' My wife told him.

" Then," he said, ' if fifty pounds is of any use he can have it at once as a loan or as a gift."

' Afterwards I met him to express my thanks. This was how he put himself alongside my work.

" I am, you see, engaged in reconstructing these premises, and in planning these I have to consider all the different departments and their relations to one another. Your problem is similar, but more complicated and on a far larger scale." '

Very soon after this good friend passed away. It was in going to his funeral that Mr. Howard came by the only accident which marred his long record of perfect health. He fell in hurrying to catch a train and was laid up for some time.

' *To-morrow*, as the book was first called, was published in October 1898 and was on the whole favourably received. *The Times* expressed a view which was pretty general :

' The only difficulty is to create such a City, but that is a small matter to Utopians.'

' In that *The Times* was mistaken. I never regarded the difficulties as small, but set myself to face them and to seek to get others far more influential than myself to face them also.

' In December 1898 I gave a lecture illustrated by lantern slides prepared by the Rev. Charter Pigott at Rectory Road Congregational Church. Mr. E. T. Young, Past-President of the Society of Actuaries, presided.

' Soon after this with the help of a few friends I formed the Garden City Association, the chief object of which was " to promote the discussion of the project suggested by Mr. Ebenezer Howard in his book, *To-morrow : A Peaceful Path to Real Reform*, and ultimately to formulate a practical scheme on the lines of that project with such modifications as may appear desirable." '

That resolution—how many of them there are—is a perfect picture of a new idea knocking at the door of the English mind, bidden to stand and answer the sentry's challenge : ' Who goes there ? ' to show passports—give the password—account for its presence. The sentries are only doing their duty, but they make progress terribly slow when the process has to be repeated thousands of times.

" Here, I may add," says Mr. Howard, " that my friends and supporters never regarded this book, any more than I did, as more than a sketch or outline of what we hoped to accomplish."

It is on record that a traveller in Ireland got out at a junction and asked a porter if he could get to Killarney from the junction. " Aye," was the reply, " but if it's Killarney you're going to I wouldn't advise you to start from where you are."

Howard was willing to start from just where he was, sure that he couldn't start from anywhere else—but he never intended to let the start limit either the route or the goal of his journey.

A typical incident of the propaganda stage when he spent a

c

"good deal of time lecturing" is preserved in one of his letters written to Mr. F. Redding, now of 17 Ridge Road, Letchworth.

*September 30th*, 1908.

DEAR SIR,

I thank you very much for your letter of the 28th, which only reached me late last evening.

When I heard from Mr. Roach that you were coming to see me and that you were, to use his words, "immensely pleased with the Garden City," I was, I can assure you, made very happy ; especially as your visit to me a little later showed me very clearly that your liking was real and sincere. For this represented more—very much more to me—than a sense that *you and your friends* were pleased ; glad as I was at that : it convinced me that *many other workpeople* would also enjoy living here. And what would that mean ? It meant that the workpeople of London, and of other overcrowded cities, would soon put into their programme a *strong demand* for more and more Garden Cities.

And now I may tell you a little incident. About ten years ago my late wife was speaking to a meeting of working women not far from your house—at Tottenham. We were even then forming a Garden City Association—just a body to talk and write about the subject and to stir the minds of men and women to its possibilities. No Garden City was then in existence ; and no money to build it either ; and no people of "influence" connected with the movement. But what we needed was a little money for propaganda work.

Well, my wife, as I say, was speaking, and after she sat down, fourteen working women each paid 1s. and became members of the Garden City Association. And one of them said to her, "We do not expect the Garden City you have talked about to come in our lifetime ; but if it comes in our children's and our grandchildren's lifetime our shillings will have been well spent."

And they *were* well spent ;—they were the *best* shillings we ever received.

Yes, the Garden City is a practical gospel for working people —aye and for all people. And every one of you who come to Letchworth, and help to build it up, and to make it a far better place than it is now, will not only reap a reward for yourselves and your children, but you will be doing a good work for all future

generations. This work is on practical lines : it is good business
for employer and employed : and it will help to make the British
Empire flourish—where it does not flourish to-day—in the homes
and lives of the great masses of the people.

With all good wishes,

Yours sincerely,

(*Signed*) EBENEZER HOWARD.

Original supplied by Mrs. Simmons, daughter of Mr. Langston, of Langston's
Patch.

Another record of this period is the first entry in the Minute
book of the Garden City Association which became an important
factor in the movement. Surely nothing could be more unassum-
ingly characteristic than this meeting of a dozen men in a city
office to start a ball rolling which was to roll round the World.
From the first the impetus which set the ball in motion comes from
Mr. Howard. When the meeting took place the men whose names
are known as makers of the history of the time were meditating
the Boer War. Which were the real makers of history ?

GARDEN CITY ASSOCIATION

MINUTES OF PROCEEDINGS

1899. *June* 10*th*

Meeting

The first meeting of the above Association was held at the offices
of Mr. Alexander W. Payne, 70 Finsbury Pavement, London, E.C.
Present : Messrs. A. Bishop, G. Crosoer, the Rev. J. Johnson, G.
King, E. Howard, J. Hyder, F. Mansford, A. Payne, W. Charter
Piggott, W. Sheowring, A. Singleton, F. Steere, and J. Bruce Wallace.

airman

Mr. Alfred Bishop was elected to the Chair.

n. Sec.

Mr. Francis W. Steere was elected Honorary Secretary *pro tem.*

. Howard

Mr. Ebenezer Howard made a statement in which he dwelt upon
the advantages and necessity of forming an Association. Each member should make it his business to enlist associates from his own neighbourhood. There were many difficulties to be overcome. Only one
of those writers who had reviewed his book had grappled really with
them. Persons who were ready to face and discuss them would be of
the greatest use in an Association of this kind. There was an absolute
necessity that many should co-operate, in order to bring in others and
aid in the dissemination of the idea.

sociation
med

Proposed by Mr. Hyder seconded by Mr. Johnson and carried
unanimously—

" That it is desirable to form an Association for promoting in its
main features, by educational and other means, the project suggested
by Mr. Ebenezer Howard in his book *To-morrow : a Peaceful Path to*

*Real Reform* and that those here present hereby constitute themselves such an Association."

Proposed by Mr. Wallace, seconded by Mr. Piggott: **Hon. Treasurer**
" That Mr. Alexander W. Payne be Honorary Treasurer *pro tem.*"
Carried.

Proposed by Mr. Johnson, seconded by Mr. Sheowring, that the **Name of Associati**
name of the Association be " Garden City Association." Carried.

The names and addresses of those present were then taken on a **List of members**
separate paper marked G.C.A. (1) to form a list of first members, the
signature of each being obtained. The following is a copy of the list,
the names being arranged alphabetically.

| Names. | Addresses. |
|---|---|
| Alfred Bishop | " Barnwood," Tunbridge Wells. |
| George Crosoer | 39 Ickleford Road, Hitchin. |
| Joseph Johnson | 80 Rectory Road, N. |
| George King | 166 Evening Road, Upper Clapton, N.E. |
| Ebenezer Howard | 50 Durley Road, Stamford Hill. |
| Joseph Hyder | 432 Strand, W.C. |
| Herbert Mansford | 53 Aldersgate Street, E.C. |
| Alexander W. Payne | 70 Finsbury Pavement, E.C. |
| W. Charter Piggott | 40 Oliphant St., Queens Park, W. |
| W. Sheowring | 24 Bethune Road, Stoke Newington. |
| A. H. Singleton | 6 Drapers' Gardens, E.C. |
| Francis W. Steere | 7 Archibald Road, Tufnell Park. |
| J. Bruce Wallace | 59 St. John's Park, N. |

Proposed by Mr. King, seconded by Mr. Wallace that Messrs. Howard, **Provisior Committ**
Johnson, Payne and Steere together with Mr. Flear of 4 Rainsbury
Road, St. Albans, be appointed a provisional Committee to form Rules
for the Association and to report to the next meeting. Carried.

Proposed by Mr. King, seconded by Mr. Hyder, that the Provisional **Next Me**
Committee be instructed to summon the next meeting of the Association
and of those in sympathy with the movement. Carried.

Proposed by Mr. King, seconded by Mr. Payne, that the next meeting
be held at Mr. Singleton's, 6 Drapers' Gardens, E.C., on Friday, June
30th, at 6 p.m.

JOHN LENG (chairman.)[1]

*30th June*, 1899.

---

[1] Sir John Leng, of Dundee.

# V

## THE BOOK—*GARDEN CITIES OF TO-MORROW*
## AND ITS INFLUENCE

He differed from his fellows as poets differ from more precise persons in
that their imaginations serve them in another capacity. The poet has no
dreams, but beautiful realities. Imagination knows no death and lives on
in a thousand bodies, sees and receives a thousand impressions to which we
under souls are senseless.

E. H.

'At the outset,' wrote Mr. Howard, 'I perceived that the first
thing was to make the project widely known—that this city which
was pictured so vividly in my own mind must be pictured more
or less vividly by many.'

He describes the Garden City that is to be as built in concentric
circles—the centre is a group of civic buildings round a campus,
midway there is a circular Grand Avenue 400 feet in width with
trees and green verges.  The outermost circle is an agricultural
belt permanently devoted to growing fruit and vegetables for the
city and supplying it with eggs and milk.  In some distant future
other garden cities may arise in the neighbourhood, but there will
then be two agricultural belts between them acting as buffers to
keep them a wholesome distance apart.  There is a manufacturing
area, several residential areas, a shopping centre and abundant
provision of playing fields.  Six boulevards radiate from the centre
much on the plan sketched for Washington, D.C., by Major L'Enfant,
which American town planners are now trying to recover from a
mass of miscellaneous buildings.  The original plan can be seen
in the sweep of Massachusetts and Connecticut Avenues as one
looks towards the Capitol.  Major L'Enfant thought of building
a majestic city fitted to be the Government capital of the United
States.  Howard was thinking of a marriage of Town and Country,
a new phase of World-civilisation, an even more ambitious
aim.

The plan outlined in the book has often been summarised ; one of the best of the thumb-nail accounts follows :—

An estate of 6,000 acres was to be bought at a cost of £40 an acre, or £240,000. The estate was to be held in trust, ' first, as a security for the debenture-holders, and, secondly, in trust for the people of Garden City.' A town was to be built near the centre of the estate to occupy about 1,000 acres. In the centre was to be a park in which were placed the public buildings, and around the park a great arcade containing shops, etc. The population of the town was to be 30,000. The building plots were to be of an average size of 20 by 130 feet. There were to be common gardens and co-operative kitchens. On the outer ring of the town there were to be factories, warehouses, etc., fronting on a circular railway. The agricultural estate of 5,000 acres was to be properly developed for agricultural purposes as part of the scheme, and the population of this belt was taken at 2,000.

The entire revenue of the town was to be derived from ground rents, which were considered to be amply sufficient (a) to pay the interest on the money with which the estate is purchased, (b) to provide a sinking fund for the purpose of paying off the principal, (c) to construct and maintain all such works as are usually constructed and maintained by municipal and other local authorities out of rates compulsorily levied, and (d) after redemption of debentures to provide a large surplus for other purposes, such as old-age pensions or insurance against accident and sickness.

The ground rents were therefore described as rate-rents. The administration of the town was to be in the hands of a Board of Management elected by the rate-renters.

Questions of finance, engineering, municipal enterprise, agriculture, local option, etc., are discussed in the book, but the essence of the scheme is contained in these words :

There are in reality not only, as is so constantly assumed, two alternatives —town life and country life—but a third alternative, in which all the advantages of the most energetic and active town life, with all the beauty and delight of the country, may be secured in perfect combination.

This " healthy, natural and economic combination of town and country life " was to be brought about by ownership of the land in the interest of the community living upon it. The town was to be properly planned, limited in size, and all the amenities of life were to be developed ; but the power of this " town-country magnet" as the author called it, came from the fact that there was to be " but one landlord, and this the community." " If the book be examined—and it is still worth careful reading—it will be found that although the details of the scheme are treated with a certain amount of hesitation, the firm basis of it is the unity of urban and

rural interests in a single community and the ownership of the
land by that community."[1] So says the introduction to *Town
Theory and Practice*, underlining the point that thirty years have
not made Howard's book out of date.

The influence of Mr. Howard's book indicates that in his aim
he was remarkably successful. He did create a " mental picture "
which must be judged in the light of its intention and its results.
It was a description and a defence of an ideal. Read to-day in the
light of later knowledge it is easy to criticise. The actual
calculations as to finance are vitiated by the fact that he
assumes a population of 30,000 as the basis of his calculations
throughout. Letchworth has about half that number of inhabitants twenty-five years after its inception. It has carried
during these years of development the institutions of a town twice
its present size. Instead of the easy profits which Mr. Howard
pictured as the normal condition of the Estate Company there
has been a narrow balance between incomings and outgoings.
Letchworth has paid its way and is slowly paying off arrears of
cumulative dividend. Meanwhile it has been discharging many
of the functions of a Garden City as outlined in the book and has
served as a working model of the ideal. Optimistic calculations
must be allowed for where the ideal anticipates the real. When
Mr. Joseph Chamberlain was pressed to justify his figures in a
Tariff campaign he replied that he merely used " figures as illustrations." As illustrations Mr. Howard's figures may be accepted.
They gave a sense of reality, calculation, business acumen to the
book which a bare statement of principles would have lacked.

Considerable prominence is given in the book to plans for a
Crystal Palace which was to be used partly for showrooms for
Garden City industries and partly as a Winter Garden. Much
ingenuity is shown in the way admission to the Crystal Palace
was to be worked as a means of trade censorship in the town. No
such institution has come into existence as yet—though there is
an arcade of shops which affords good shelter on a stormy Saturday
night to crowds of young people.

Details of this kind are important in actual town building but
not really important in a book. In the main the book gains by
keeping to principles. There is verve and force in it : it carries

[1] *Town Theory and Practice*, by Lethaby, Unwin, Pepler, Chambers, Reiss and
Purdom. Published by Benn Brothers.

LETCHWORTH—THE SPIRELLA FACTORY

the reader along with a swing, and at the end he is aware that it has confronted him with a new idea. The idea is nothing less than a vision of a transformed English industrial civilisation. No revolution has taken place. It is a 'peaceful pathway to real reform.' The ordinary machinery of Parliament is adequate to give the enabling powers necessary. There is no antagonism to any class. Landlords are not regarded as worse than any other people. There is no 'waiting till some party is in power.' No abolition of anything in particular except slum dwellings and over-crowded industrial districts, and these disappear like a dissolving view. The migration of industrial population into the country takes place within the usual forms of law and by the usual methods of road and rail, motors and trains. Factories,—no longer 'dark Satanic mills'—have become sightly buildings standing in gardens. Workmen's dwellings have become sanitary and attractive, each in its own ground or situated round plots of common turf. Derelict farms have been reoccupied because there is a market at their doors. Rent and rates have become less of a strain on the workers' budget, vegetables and fruit have become available without going further than the kitchen garden. A transvaluation of values has somehow been effected. Where foxes and partridges had been the principal occupiers of land in parks and preserves the land is carrying its complement of modest homes ; red-cheeked children have taken the place of bright plumaged birds. England is looking sober, prosperous, thrifty—as though the bad dream of the industrial revolution had somehow had no more permanence than any other 'fabric of a vision.' The dream is broken, the ugly nineteenth century has been wiped off the slate and the country has resumed its natural evolution from the eighteenth century, allowing for the changes necessitated by discoveries of science and improvements in the art of living.

'There is a broad path open through a creation of *new wealth forms*, to a new industrial system in which the productive forces of a society and of nature may be used with far greater effectiveness than at present, and in which the distribution of the wealth forms so created will take place on a far juster and more equitable basis.'

This is the real thesis of Howard's book. Many references to it overlook its main purpose. They regard it as the book that founded Letchworth as though that were its aim. But Letchworth was only an illustration of the "*new wealth forms to be created.*"

It was an experiment, a sample, a test, an effort to " try out " the new idea and see whether it were as good in practice as it was in idea. The purchase of a second estate at Welwyn and the foundation of Welwyn Garden City are proof enough that Howard himself had he lived for another fifty years would not have felt that his mission was accomplished by establishing one Garden City or two. What he wanted was a movement—a corporate migration out of overcrowded cities into green pastures. Not comfortable people making themselves more comfortable in better surroundings, but battalions, companies and squads of working folk shaking off the spell of the slums, the germs, the smoke, the smells, the sombre atmosphere, the unprofitable leisure and unwholesome work which are inseparable from unregulated industrialism in over-populated districts. Industrial England had descended into Hell—though the terminus had other names in the railway time-tables. *Garden Cities of To-morrow* was to open the gates of the prison house and the ransomed were to return to their lost privileged estate.

Mr. Howard's vision gave him a clear picture of how this transformation was to take place. First a Garden City as a working model. Then a group of garden cities each of about 50,000 inhabitants. Then clusters of garden cities covering the Home Counties round London. Then the rebuilding of London itself when the inhabitants had some alternative place to go to during the process of rebuilding.

The book in fact closes with this bold leap into the future. ' The time for the complete reconstruction of London has not yet come. It will eventually take place on a far more comprehensive scale than that now exhibited in Paris, Berlin, Glasgow, Birmingham or Vienna.' [New York with the Bronx and Westchester Parkways may now be included in the list.] ' But a simpler problem must first be solved. One small Garden City must be built as a working model and then a group of cities. These tasks done and done well the reconstruction of London must inevitably follow.'

It is characteristic of the attitude of Mr. Howard's mind that, faced with the difficulties incident to a transformation so thoroughgoing as this, he does not propose any new legislation—not even the creation of a Garden City Party in the House of Commons. It is all to come about by the attraction of the better way, the creation of new values which will be more attractive than the old.

' Some of my friends have suggested that such a scheme of town clusters is well enough adapted to a new country, but that in an old-settled country, with its towns built and its railway system for the most part constructed, it is quite a different matter.  But surely to raise such a point is to contend, in other words, that the existing wealth forms of the country are permanent, and are for ever to serve as hindrances to the introduction of better forms ; that crowded, ill-ventilated, unplanned, unwieldy, unhealthy cities —ulcers on the very face of our beautiful island—are to stand as barriers to the introduction of towns in which modern scientific methods and the aims of social reformers may have the fullest scope in which to express themselves.  No, it cannot be ; at least, it cannot be for long.  What Is may hinder What Might Be for a while, but cannot stay the tide of progress.  These crowded cities have done their work ; they were the best which a society largely based on selfishness, acquisitiveness and fear could construct, but they are in the nature of things entirely unadapted for a society in which the social side of our nature is demanding a larger share of recognition—a society where even the very love of self leads us to insist upon a greater regard for the well-being of our fellows. The large cities of to-day are scarcely better adapted for the expression of the fraternal spirit than would a work on astronomy which taught that the earth was the centre of the universe be capable of adaptation for use in our schools.  Each generation should build to suit its own needs ; and it is no more in the nature of things that men should continue to live in old areas because their ancestors lived in them, than it is that they should cherish the old beliefs which a wider faith and a more enlarged understanding have outgrown.  The reader is, therefore, earnestly asked not to take it for granted that the large cities in which he may perhaps take a pardonable pride are necessarily, in their present form, any more permanent than the stage-coach system which was the subject of so much admiration just at the very moment when it was about to be supplanted by the railways.[1]  The simple issue to be faced, and faced resolutely, is : ' Can better results be obtained by starting on a bold plan on comparatively virgin soil than by attempting to adapt our old cities to our newer and higher needs ?  Thus fairly faced, the question can only be answered in one way ; and when that simple fact is well grasped, the social

[1] See, for instance, the opening chapter of *The Heart of Midlothian* (Sir Walter Scott).

revolution will speedily commence.' No one knows better than those who have set their hands to slum clearance that the logical, economic, and hygienic way—the only way which promises ultimate success—is to buy land where land is cheap and open up an alternative residential area under conditions which make slumdom impossible. That conclusion is the vindication of Mr. Howard's insight.

# VI

# THE RAPTURE OF THE FORWARD VIEW

The inspired personality is one in whom some hidden force, idea, or impulse becomes an incandescent flame affording light to others.

*Professor A. C. Bradley.*

To understand how the book brought together a great variety of forward interests in England one has to relive in imagination the eighties and nineties of last century. Social enthusiasm ran high. Henry George's *Progress and Poverty* had made a deep impression and left behind it societies for Land Nationalisation. Mr. Joseph Chamberlain had his campaign on the three F's. His star shone brilliant in the sky as the Messiah of radical England. Ruskin's economics with their wholly ideal resuscitation of ethical principles in industry were working beneath the surface like a leaven. Herbert Spencer had formulated a doctrine of social evolution which appeared to fit present facts into a hopeful scheme for the future. Arnold Toynbee had given his name to Toynbee Hall and there was a steady movement for the establishment of University settlements. The facts about sweating, overcrowding, unemployment and casual employment, endemic diseases and drink were filtering into the drawing-rooms of the West End. Cardinal Manning had been called in to arbitrate in the Dock Strike. John Burns had been incarcerated for a speech in Trafalgar Square. The Fabians were meeting and talking. W. T. Stead brought out General Booth's *Darkest England and the Way Out.* Bellamy's *Looking Backward* had a great run. The Christian Social Union was founded in Oxford—Nonconformists excluded. Father Adderly wrote and preached on the condition of the people and Canon Scott Holland threw a generous ægis over the *Commonwealth.* Sidney and Mrs. Webb fired off statistics like bullets from a machine gun. The Labour Church broke out like an epidemic in industrial centres. The foundations of the Labour Party were laid. Mr. Lloyd George's oratory kindled hopes that the mantle of the radical Joseph Cham-

berlain had fallen on a successor. Ruskin Hall was established in
Oxford by Mr. Walter Vrooman to supply the movement with
leaders economically equipped for their task. Blatchford's *Merrie
England* ran into many thousands of copies. The *Clarion* came
out week by week written with fervent enthusiasm, pungent satire,
in admirably clear, resonant and forceful English, and was read
with devout response by thousands of young men and women who
discussed it in their *Clarion* clubs.

Alongside this yeasty ferment of economic discontent there was
an æsthetic revolt against Victorian traditions in the sacred name
of beauty. People began to realise that a London suburb was
not the last word in civilisation. London itself began to look like
a village which had suffered from elephantiasis. Matthew Arnold
with his Mr. Bottles and Coles Truss Factory in Trafalgar Square,
standing where it ought not, made Londoners look twice at Trafalgar
Square and turn away with a smile and a shrug of the shoulders.
Town Councillors looked up their dictionaries to see the meaning
of words like symmetry, perspective, harmony, applied to the
architecture of their Market Street and High Street. Wordsworth's
sonnets were much quoted in sermons and speeches. There were
many signs that England was becoming beauty-conscious, not
merely with reverence for ancient and immemorial beauty, but with
the desire to create new forms of beauty in close association with life.

Pulpits, both Anglican and Free, expressed the newly discovered
social conscience. "In the England of forty years ago," writes
Dean Inge in *Christian Ethics and Social Problems*, "the idea of a
secularised Kingdom of God, to be realised in the near future, took
a strong hold of religious minds. The contrasts between wealth
and poverty were more glaring then than they are now, and woman's
labour especially was cruelly sweated. It would not be possible
to paint such a dark picture to-day as some of our eloquent preachers
gave us, not without exaggeration, but true in the main, in Queen
Victoria's reign. It is only fair to give some credit to religious
leaders like Maurice, Kingsley, and Barnett for stirring the public
conscience, and in the next generation to the members of the
Christian Social Union, such as Westcott, Scott Holland and Bishop
Gore for carrying on their work." Mansfield House, Canning Town,
the Whitecross Street Settlement of the Methodists, the Browning
Settlement in Walworth gave expression to the same spirit in the
Free Churches.

LETCHWORTH—SMALL HOLDING, BALDOCK ROAD, LOOKING TOWARDS HOUSE

It is only in the light of this widespread social interest and enthusiasm that we can understand how a book written by an unknown man came to create first a Garden City and ultimately a movement which has had its repercussions in every civilised country in the world.

There was something for every kind of idealist in Howard's plan. There was a chance of self-realisation in a new sphere which pleased the individualist. There was a corporate life, a co-operative endeavour, a communal ideal which pleased the socialist. People who had suffered under London landlords read with avidity of a town where the town-site would be publicly owned and the un-earned increment would accrue to the inhabitants. Manufacturers saw in it a chance of increasing the real wages, i.e. the comfort and health, of their employees without attempting impossible changes in the economic system. Workmen with ailing children saw a chance of doing better for their families than they had been able to do for themselves. Temperance reformers seized upon the scheme as an opportunity of creating a township without a public house. People who were hankering to get "back to the land" were eager to secure a small holding. A few who had heard whispers of a new-old art—the art of town-planning—felt that their hour had come. Fortunately a few magicians of finance like Mr. William Lever (Lord Leverhulme) and George Cadbury saw an opportunity of discharging a social duty and at the same time finding employment for superfluous capital.

There is a sturdy backbone of Puritanism in England largely represented by members of the Society of Friends. Numbers of people of this type gravitated to the Garden City in the hope of realising the simpler life as described by Emerson. "To live content with small means : to seek elegance rather than luxury : and refinement rather than fashion : to be worthy, not respectable : and wealthy not rich : to study hard : think quietly : talk gently : act frankly : to listen to stars and birds, to babes and sages with open heart : to bear all cheerfully, do all bravely, await occasions, hurry never. In a word to let the spiritual unbidden and unconscious grow up through the common."

One of the venerable ideals of Christianity sees it as a clean, plain, orderly life of work, leisure and devotion in an associated community, and this has survived all the shocks of modernism. The ideal was expressed by St. Bernard for his Cistercians : "Bonum est nos hic esse quia homo vivit purius, cadet rarius, surgit velocius, incedit cautius, quiescit securius, moriturus felicius, purgator citius, praemiatur copiosus." Wordsworth has versified the Latin in words which no one has yet ventured to apply to the Garden City although they might well be adopted as a statement of its religious ideal :

> Here man more purely lives, less oft doth fall,
> More promptly rises, walks with nicer heed
> More safely rests, dies happier, is freed
> Earlier from cleansing fires and gains withal
> A brighter crown . . .
> A gentler life spreads round the holy spires
> Where'er they rise, the sylvan waste retires
> And aery harvests crown the fertile lea.

Nothing can make an ideal of this kind out of date—religion incarnated in life. Religion must always have more in it than gets into any life, but when the ideal is held fast the life will be so in harmony with the religion that it does not exclude fuller development.

It is no small tribute to the genuineness of these enthusiasms that a scheme which promised no prospect of immediate financial advantage to anyone drew like a magnet men of such varied interests and such different qualities. We may ask whether there is any other product of that stormy seed time which can compare with the Garden City and Town Planning Movement for sincerity, sanity, success, and promise of the future.

### § RAPID PROGRESS

Who is the great man ? He is great who inspires others to think for themselves, who shocks you, irritates you, affronts you, so that you are jostled out of your wonted ways, pulled out of your mental ruts, lifted out of the mire of the commonplaces which you alternately love and hate.

*Elbert Hubbard.*

Events moved rapidly after Mr. Howard's book was published. The time was ripe and many who had been thinking over the subject saw that this was the opportunity for making an effort to deal with it. As the difference between Howard's book and many that had preceded it was that the ideals of *Garden Cities of To-morrow* were translated into realities, and the others remained in the sphere of the ideal, it is important to trace the intermediate steps in this case. If the intermediate steps were not all of Mr. Howard's

D

devising they indicate that he had an instinct for the right way of giving effect to his plans.

## 1898

Publication of *To-morrow : A Peaceful Path to Real Reform*, re-issued in 1902 under the title *Garden Cities of To-morrow*. Contrast the concrete effect of this title with Sir Benjamin Ward's *Hygeia* and James Silk Buckingham's *National Evils and Practical Remedies*.

## 1899

Eight months after the publication of the book a Garden City Association was formed. The object of the Association was to carry on the discussion of Mr. Howard's project by means of lectures, and " ultimately to formulate a practical scheme on the lines of the project with such modifications as may seem desirable." The first Honorary Secretary was Mr. F. W. Steere, a barrister. He was followed by Mr. Clement M. Bailhache, afterwards Mr. Justice Bailhache. Mr. Howard writes : " Whatever else may be in doubt this is certain—that the Garden City took its rise in the minds and hearts of those who were strongly in favour of the public ownership of land. The Garden City Association was born in the offices of Mr. Alex. Payne, Treasurer of the Land Nationalisation Society : its first meeting was presided over by Mr. Alfred Bishop, long an ardent supporter of the movement : one of its first Honorary Secretaries (Mr. Steere) was also Honorary Secretary of the Land Nationalisation Society : and the Chairman of the Board of Directors of First Garden City Ltd. was the Chairman of the Executive of the Land Nationalisation Society. Three months after the formation Mr. Howard was able to declare : " The Association numbers among its members manufacturers, co-operators, architects, artists, medical men, financial experts, lawyers, merchants, ministers of religion, members of the London County Council (Moderate and Progressive) Socialists and Individualists, Radicals and Conservatives."

Committees were appointed to consider the problems with which the new town would have to deal—land tenure, housing, labour, engineering, architecture, education, liquor traffic, and manufactures. The " Sites Committee " got busy inspecting sites, and intensive propaganda was set going.

## May, 1900

The Association resolved " To form a limited company called
the *Garden City Limited* with a share capital of £50,000 of which
£5,000 was to be a first issue, with a cumulative 5 per cent dividend,
' redeemable at the option of a body of trustees representing inhabitants, provided that when so redeemed holders of shares receive
a premium of 10 per cent in addition to any cumulative interest.' "

## 1901

Mr. Ralph Neville, K.C., became Chairman of the Council, and
Mr. Thomas Adams, a young eneregtic and practical Scot, was
appointed its first paid Secretary.   A conference was organised at
Mr. Cadbury's village, Bournville, and was attended by three
hundred delegates from Borough and Urban District Councils,
trade unions, co-operative and friendly societies.

## 1902

A second Conference was held at Port Sunlight near Liverpool
—Mr. W. H. Lever's proprietary model town.   This was attended
by a thousand delegates of public bodies and societies, indicating
that the Garden City Movement had captured the imagination of
a large public.

## June, 1902

There was a meeting in the Crown Room, Holborn Restaurant,
with Earl Grey in the Chair.   After hearing speeches from Mr.
Ralph Neville, Mr. W. H. Lever, Sir William Richmond, the Bishops
of Rochester and Hereford and Mr. Aneurin Williams, approval
was given to the formation of a PIONEER Company with the definite
object of securing a site and preparing a scheme for the development of a Garden City.

## July, 1902

The Garden City Pioneer Company was registered with a Capital
of £20,000.   The memorandum of Association sets forth the object
of the Company as follows :
" To promote and further the distribution of the industrial
population on the land on the lines suggested in Mr. Ebenezer
Howard's book entitled *Garden Cities of To-morrow*, and to examine,
test, and obtain information, advice, and assistance with regard

ESTATE OFFICE AND BANK, LETCHWORTH

to the matters therein contained, with the view of forming in any part of the United Kingdom *Garden Cities*, that is to say, towns or settlements for agricultural, industrial, commercial and residential purposes, or any of them, in accordance with Mr. Howard's scheme, or any modifications thereof."

Ralph Neville, K.C., is Chairman. The Directors are Edward Cadbury, Ebenezer Howard, T. H. W. Idris, Howard D. Pearsall, Franklin Thomasson, Thomas Purvis Ritzema, Aneurin Williams.

It is interesting to note that the purposes of the Company are much wider than the formation of one Garden City. They cover the contingencies of a national movement. The whole of the £20,000 was subscribed before December 1902, about four months after the issue of the prospectus.

### April, 1903

Through Mr. Herbert Warren of Messrs. Balderston & Warren, the Company heard of the Letchworth estate near Hitchin in Hertfordshire. Within a year from the foundation of the Company contracts were signed for the purchase of the greater part of the estate and shortly afterwards the purchase of the whole area was completed. The land was bought from fifteen different owners at a total cost of £155,587. The area—since increased—was 3,818 acres, so that the average cost per acre was £40 15s. The purchase from individual owners without anyone knowing the whole plan was an epic of skilful management.

### September 1, 1903

First Garden City Ltd. was registered at Somerset House with an authorised capital of £300,000 and seven days later the first prospectus was issued inviting subscriptions for £80,000 share capital.

### October 9, 1903

Earl Grey presided over a formal opening of the First Garden City at Letchworth. A thousand shareholders and other guests attended a meeting which was to celebrate the beginning of a new movement in a county which had a thousand years of recorded history.

The Pioneer Company, having done its work so well, was wound up seventeen months after its formation.

# VII

## RECRUITS: SIR RALPH NEVILLE

*As builders of cities we English are more ignominious than rabbits.*
*D. H. Lawrence.*

As an expert stenographer working in the Courts, Howard had become well known to both barristers and judges. They read his book from interest in him, and attracted by the soundness of his plan they became interested in the Garden City movement for its own sake. Among them was Mr. Ralph Neville, K.C., afterwards a Judge of His Majesty's High Court. His personality and his interpretation of the movement were conspicuous reinforcements. There was nothing woolly about Mr. Neville's mind. He knew what he wanted and why he wanted it, and he expressed his views as a judge may do as though it bordered on a misdemeanour to doubt or question them. His mind had the philosophic background of a man who had thought seriously about the nature of the institutions he administered. There is an afterglow of an intelligent enthusiasm for Herbert Spencer's evolutionary conception of human history reflected in his statement of the place and function of garden cities. His addresses contain an incipient philosophy of the movement which is a useful addendum to Howard's own statement.

He starts from the axiom that the human race is subject to natural law. The law operates impartially. If we work in harmony with it, it promotes development, producing progressively improving results. If we do not adjust our way of living to natural law the consequence is seen in various stages of degeneration. Degeneration is as much a law of nature as evolution. The law is not a "fiat" issued by an autocrat. It is an observed sequence which we discover by noting maladjustments of human society and tracing them to their source.

> Man, like a pebble on a glacier,
> Moves imperceptibly, but always down.

44

LETCHWORTH—CHILDREN'S PADDLING POOL IN HOWARD PARK ; MEMORIAL STONE ON RIGHT

[1] ' Hitherto in the management of his own existence man has in his ignorance disregarded laws of health in the pursuit of his business, his ambition and his appetites. His habits of life with regard to dwellings, food and drink have been formed without reference to their effect on his physique and much evil and suffering has resulted. If having violated Nature's laws he had left her to avenge herself Nature would in her straightforward and relentless fashion have thrust out and exterminated the victims of unhealthy habits and reckless living. But man, though he cannot with impunity defy the laws of Nature, can and does habitually modify their operation. Having by misapplication of our intelligence rendered a large proportion of the community physically unfit, we proceed by further application of our intelligence to ensure that the unfit shall have as good a chance of survival as the fit. We first get into trouble by ignoring natural law, then stand between Nature and the remedy she would have applied. This makes the study of Sociology a necessity. We must strive to build our civilisation on a basis which will not involve the manufacture of victims of ill living, and their subsequent rescue at the cost of the general welfare. What in the past was a blunder has in the light of present knowledge become a crime. We have to find the right conditions of social life and establish them, or take the consequences, and the penalty of failure is extinction.

' Natural law is manifesting itself in industrial England chiefly by physical deterioration, and though mental and moral deterioration may be checked by other factors both intellectual and moral, development must be based on sound physique if they are to be permanent. The principal cause of physical deterioration is the congestion of population in our large towns, which are amorphous masses of seething humanity put to shame by the domestic policy of the ant and the bee. We cannot reverse the policy which has led capital to seek investment in industries. That is equally a necessity for the community, the capitalist, and for labour. But we can extricate industries from the unwholesome and repulsive environment in which they are carried on and set them down in pure air, beautiful surroundings and hygienic conditions. The patching up of old towns is a second best—why not

[1] Précis from *Some Papers and Addresses on Social Questions*, by the late Sir Ralph Neville, with preface by Sir Alfred Hopkinson. Spottiswood, Ballantyne & Co., Ltd.

provide for new towns, not growing haphazard as they do now, but built on a definite plan for a definite purpose ? '

This leads to a description of the situation and plan of Letchworth as a type of a new residential town.

Advocacy of this kind was sufficiently novel and impressive to justify the selection of Mr. Ralph Neville as Chairman of the First Garden City Company when it was formed.

Looking back upon it now and contrasting his clear vision of town planning with the lack of co-ordination which has created Sloughs of Despond in various parts of Southern England since the War, and has given us factories without housing in one place and houses without factories in another, one can only wonder at the courage and farsightedness which made one of His Majesty's Judges identify himself with a movement which thirty years later has still to encounter a dead-weight of misunderstanding and inertia. His adhesion to the movement was a turning point in its history. People who were hesitating as to the project came in because they had confidence in Neville and believed he knew what he was about. It would be invidious and perhaps misleading to mention names in chronological sequence. The important fact was that when Neville became Chairman his known integrity and intellectual weight made people feel that the Garden City Company represented a serious movement which had to be reckoned with.

The following appreciation by Ebenezer Howard indicates the value he set on Justice Neville's support.

' Experience has taught me that it is rare to find a successful public man—especially one who is still mounting the ladder—who is willing to identify himself closely and actively with a movement which is in its infancy—especially if that movement be regarded as visionary and impracticable ; for to do this may involve grave risk, and a reputation which has been hard to win may be easily lost.

' But Mr. Ralph Neville, K.C.,—as he was in 1901—was far too big a man to be influenced by considerations of this kind. His judgment was sound and independent, and he quite wisely relied upon it ; his heart was warm, and he allowed it a proper share with his brain in the guidance of his life. In short, he had but to be convinced that a course was right, and he at once decided to pursue it, regardless of personal consequences.

'In 1901, I had already seen much of Mr. Neville, for I had taken shorthand notes of his speeches and his examination of witnesses at the High Court, and had become impressed with his great ability and his rare fairness. So, when in March of that year I found that he had been endorsing the proposals of the Garden City Association in *Labour Co-partnership*, I felt "Now our movement will go ahead, for we shall secure a truly doughty and courageous Chairman."

'In an article Mr. Neville had said: "Without pledging myself to every detail—for we still await lessons of experience—it may be confidently asserted that the idea is based upon sound economic principle. In the increment in the value of town lands lies a huge fund hitherto carelessly given away, which, if wisely utilised, might enable the inhabitants of a town to combine in a great measure the advantages of a country life with that of town life, and while offering specially favourable conditions to industry, might raise the standard of existence among the population to an almost incalculable degree."

'After reading this article I at once called at his chambers in Old Square. He received me most cordially, and at once agreed to join the Association. He soon became Chairman of its Council, and took an active and prominent part in a movement which up till then had progressed indeed but all too slowly. For up to this time the Garden City Association had no paid Secretary, and only a share in an office, kindly lent by the Land Nationalisation Society. But now, with Mr. Neville's generous help, and relying too on a promise of substantial support secured to us through Mr. Clement Bailhache (our then hon. Secretary, now a judge of the High Court) we were able to take offices in Chancery Lane and to set about finding a secretary who would be able to devote his whole time to the work; and we were fortunate to secure in this capacity a man who has been a tower of strength to the movement—Mr. Thomas Adams, now so well known throughout this country and abroad.'

# VIII

## THE IDEALIST AT WORK

What hand and brain went ever paired ?
What heart alike conceived and dared ?
What act proved all its thought had been ?
What will but felt the fleshly screen ?

*Robert Browning.*

The first Christians were full of incredible courage; always in trouble in consequence; and nevertheless always gay and overflowing with joy.

*Dean Church.*

THIS book is a study of an idealist who was successful in getting his ideals adopted. But to appreciate his success account must be taken of the snags which beset an idealist's path. The " nigger in the wood pile " waiting for the idealist in social affairs is that when he gets to work to translate his ideal into hard fact he finds a concrete situation already in possession of the field. There is no escape from this difficulty. Men like the late Joseph Fels, the enthusiastic single taxer, have crossed the ocean to secure freedom for an experiment; but when he went to Alabama to found the new town of " Fairhope " near Mobile, U.S.A., it was only to find a different kind of concrete situation from the one he had left, providing the obstacles which his ideal had to overcome. This does not mean that the idealist is one of those who

Went out to battle but they always fell.

It does mean that his task is longer and his belief in the ideal must be stronger than most people imagine.

The trouble is inherent in the very human fact that an ideal is something we have not yet tried—otherwise it would not be an ideal—and the vast majority of people only feel confident for action when they are doing again what they have done before. If ten men are agreed on the statement of a common ideal it is probable

49

that each of them is thinking of achieving it in a different way—
the way he or his father before him has trodden.

This is one source of what is often called the tragedy of the idealist
—the distance between the bright vision of the possible and the
drab appearance of an actual which looks like its poor relation.
An artist knows that his best picture is an inadequate presentation
of the vision of beauty that inspired him to paint it.   A musician
tastes the tragedy of the ideal when he first hears the symphony
he planned for an orchestra rendered by a barrel-organ in the street.
A statesman senses the tragedy when he sees what queer and un-
expected abuses grow out of his carefully thought-out legislation.
Alice in Wonderland playing croquet with flamingoes for mallets
and hedgehogs for balls is a comic picture of the confusion made
by human wills invited to " play a game " without taking the
trouble to understand the rules.   Jacob, thinking to marry Rachel
and waking in the morning to find " behold it was Leah," is the
historic parable of the idealist's tragedy.

The problem being set by inherent limitations of human nature,
the test of the idealist comes, not when he flings his ideal out on
the world like a boomerang, but when it comes back to him in
the form of legal definitions, newspaper criticism, committee meetings, accounts, partners and disciples.   There have been idealists
who when they saw what they had started fled and hid themselves.

When the Letchworth Estate had been purchased, the First
Garden City Company formed, and the Capital subscribed, Mr.
Howard had to face the test of bringing his ideal to bear on a concrete situation.   The ideal was the fine product of twentieth-
century thinking : the concrete situation was the eighteenth century in rural England—for it is hardly an exaggeration to say that
in North Hertfordshire the nineteenth century had never occurred.
It had been, perhaps mercifully, skipped.   Frederic Seebohm had
found there his examples of the primitive village communities and
their agriculture of Saxon and Norman times, of which he wrote
so well.   The Icknield Way which crossed the Estate had been
little disturbed since Rome withdrew its legions.   Hitchin, the
North-Hertfordshire metropolis, had its eyes steadily fixed on an
illustrious past.   If it could have ignored this " so-called twentieth
century " it would have gone on dreaming pleasant dreams of days
gone by, aided by the magic wand of Mr. Reginald Hine.   " As it was
in the beginning is now and ever shall be " might have been the

motto of the part of the country where Letchworth was to come into existence.

Stories are still told of the first contact and conflict of two civilisations—the efforts of farmers and labourers to say what they thought of the " new colony " with an inadequate vocabulary of expletives—the incredulity of railway men who suspected that Letchworth would disappear in a night, the prophecies of disaster, the laughter in inns and cottages over things said by " ladies from Lunnon " to whom the commonest events of country life were new, strange, and regrettable.

This stage of Letchworth's history is epitomised in the story of its relations with Hitchin—hardly to be told by any citizen of Letchworth without raising suspicion of vainglorious satisfaction. Yet the story is worth telling because it is typical. The same indignant rejection of change, repulsion from something new, has been repeated in every part of England and still goes on ; recalling the tale of the Scottish minister faced by a demand for an organ to replace the traditional precentor :

" Weel, ma freens, there is nae doubt it would be an improvement, but all improvements are innovations, and all innovations are by all means to be resisted."

The record comes best from the local historian of Hitchin whose loyalty to the town he has commemorated is above suspicion. Mr. Reginald Hine, speaking to the Rotary clubs of Hitchin and Letchworth in February 1932, tells how indignant contempt gradually gave way to mutual respect.

' It would be a pity,' he said, ' if anything obscured the mutual history of Hitchin and Letchworth, their actions and reactions, their enmities and their friendships, their divisions and their meetings, throughout the thirty years of their acquaintance. It is an interesting, almost a fascinating story, because here you have side by side, a royal and ancient town carrying the weight of a thousand years upon its shoulders, and another town just stepping out of its cradle. You have here the meeting of opposites, the conflict, and the possibility of finding a common denominator between the old world and the new. Now it seems to me that there are four principal evolutionary stages to be observed in the relationships of these two parishes.

' The first is primitive and brutal. It marks the instinctive animosity of neighbours, as shown in the conduct of Hitchin town and Letchworth village in the old, far-off days, before the civilising effect of a Garden City had made itself known between us. We were enjoined by Holy Church to love our neighbours as ourselves. Instead of that we hated one another like poison at first sight. I will not dwell on this period. It is not creditable to either of us.

' The second stage concerns the hostile attitude of Hitchin at the foundation and during the first and crucially testing years of the Garden City. On that also I do not think it right to dwell. It is not a very honourable episode in the life of Hitchin town. We have lived to be rather ashamed of it.

' In fairness to myself and my own people, I will venture to say that our attitude, however unbecoming, was not without justification. We were a proud people. By reason of our royal and ancient history we had some reason to be proud : and our days had been long in the land. Can you wonder that we, who had wrestled for a thousand years with the overwhelming difficulties of making a town fit for Christian folk to live in should have disliked the cocksure dexterity of these new-fangled strangers who undertook to build a city in a single generation ? In the fifties and sixties we had endured, indeed we had enjoyed, the eccentricities of the Rev. John Alington, of Letchworth Hall. But here was a whole colony of eccentrics making an exhibition of themselves rather too near our sacred borders. We wished they would remove their mad city a little nearer Arlesey.[1]

' Now and again, we had a fairer notion of what it was these pioneers had set themselves to do. As we listened to the speeches at their inaugural meeting, some of us felt that we had been vouchsafed a vision of the chosen people. " They wandered in the wilderness in a solitary way ; they found no city to dwell in . . . and He led them forth by the right way that they might go to a city of habitation. . . . Oh ! that men would praise the Lord for His goodness, for His wonderful works to the children of men."

' If they were not " the chosen people " they were at least men and women of high seriousness, not content with a mean and jocular life, but deeply concerned at the drift and downward eddy of what they held to be an evil economic system. There was a ring of sincerity and a stern resolve about their articles of association. They evidently intended to find a simpler way of living on

[1] The Three Counties Asylum.

this old and complicated earth. They were tired of "the Atlantean load of all the world's affairs." They meant to carve out new thoroughfares for sad humanity to tread.

'But in the eyes of Hitchin people that vision faded all too soon. To be quite frank we were jealous of these pioneers. They might increase and we at Hitchin might decrease. We called them dreamers, and hoped that the dawn might soon come and shatter all their dreams. But they were more awake than we were. We concentrated our eyes in disgust upon their sandals and forgot to notice that these men had heads. We gazed on the great roads they built and hoped they would never lead to anywhere; we did not believe that their waterworks would hold water; we trusted that their gas reservoirs would burst.

'I have heard it said that, in this period also, Letchworthians knew how to answer back. But in the Letchworth records I see little trace of it; the reciprocity, as the Irishman said, was all upon one side. "Some men hold their tongues because they have naught to answer; and some keep silent knowing their time." There, in that last phrase, you have the truth of the whole matter. So far as I can see, the good people of Letchworth took little or no heed of the abuse that came pouring in from Hitchin. They quietly went on building. They considered the end. They listened, if at all, in that preoccupied silence which is the unbearable repartee.

'Since the world began, it has always been so with such as set out to build a city. These pioneers knew—for had it not been prophesied?—that they also would "become a prey and derision to the heathen round about." They knew that 'a city that is set on a hill cannot be hid'; and that every mistake of theirs would be magnified. It mattered not. The Hitchin people might make sport of them; they might endeavour to unbuild the city with their scorn; they might call it a city without foundations. But the pioneers had the comfortable assurance that they were building on the rock of faith, and they quietly built on.

'I said that one can trace no answering back. But one does observe a certain amused tolerance on the part of these progressive pioneers, very galling to us grave citizens of Hitchin. They made us feel that we were a peevish people and "a petty town of no import." Aware of what they intended to make of their own city, they could afford to smile at our moth-eaten community, which

LETCHWORTH—THE GRAMMAR SCHOOL AND TOWN SQUARE

ought—as one of them said—to have been decently interred a
century before, and which was amusing its dotage by making
lavender water to counteract the stench of its tanneries.

' Towards the close of this second stage, one begins to trace a
mixture of envy in the unneighbourly regard of Hitchin.   In spite
of all affronts, the experiment of this man Ebenezer Howard was
beginning to make good.   His dream was coming true.   We should
have to take these Utopians seriously after all.   With the rest of
my brethren I continued to make sport ; but it was with a doubting, half-converted heart.   There is a touch of admiration, as well
as envy, in the ironical congratulation which I wrote at the founding of Letchworth Museum.   " A praiseworthy and laudable project," I said, " to build a museum when as yet you have nothing
to put in it but yourselves."   You can trace the same feeling at
work in my father's satire about the early numbers of " that rag
they call the ' Citizen.' "   " It has nothing whatever to say," he
remarked, " but it says it uncommonly well."   And, between the
lines, you may faintly detect the same better-natured spirit in those
bantering verses which I wrote in dishonour of Garden Cities :

> God the first garden made,
> And the first city Cain,
> Deep in a proverb thus 'twas laid,
> Profound, precise and plain.
> But garden-cities, garden-cities !
> Who the deuce makes garden-cities ?
> Will someone please explain ?
> It is indeed a thousand pities
> They do not say in these old ditties ;
> For then we'd know, for weal or woe,
> Whence all these mad mixed-blessings flow,
> And folk would be no more perplext
> With that dark thought they are now vext,
> Is God or Man to blame ?

' The day after I published that malicious rhyme I received a
post card from Ebenezer Howard.   " You need not blame God,"
he wrote ; " if anyone, it is I who am to blame.   I promise to do
better next time."   That was ever the way with that enlightened
man.   Though his dream had more than half come true, he was
still the dreamer, and still the pioneer.   His Garden City of To-
morrow was never the Garden City of To-day.   He had the dis-
satisfaction of a true man of genius.   He never sank into an old

E

age of content. He was always looking forward, pressing forward, piercing the mist of the future with his prophetical, practical eyes and muttering to his faithful heart, " Next time, next time."

' Let us now pass on to the third stage, which, roughly computed, covers the period from the close of the Great War up to or towards these present times. It is a period of mutual respect, when, the clash of opposites being ended, the two towns began to explore what was civically sound in one another, and to make notes of it for their own use and imitation. It was good to have reached that stage. Recrimination may relieve the spleen, but it does not console the heart and it makes bad neighbours. In the end one wearies of it, because one feels that, if God bears with the very worst of us, we may surely endure one another.

' Apart from that Christian conviction, the Hitchin people found that the shafts of their satire no longer reached their mark. There was less and less to make fun of. When the *Daily Mail* sent down to inquire in 1910, there was hardly an eccentric left ; after a prolonged search, one man in sandals and a Roman toga was discovered, and seven of the natives speaking Esperanto as though it were a sacred language. But the chief reason why bad feeling disappeared was the remarkable success of the First Garden City. In the face of that accomplished fact the continuance of hostilities seemed petty and absurd.

' At this point one would like to pause and pay one's tribute to a work so finely achieved ; a work of singular difficulty and magnitude, and of service, by way of example, to the world at large. It has been said that there is no really great hope which was not once a forlorn hope ; and we have lived to see that almost impossible hope brought to pass. There is no need to retell a story so well known. But the thing is still marvellous in our eyes. We have seen a village become a city. We have seen fifty people multiply into fifteen thousand. We have watched a parish council that hardly ever met develop into an Urban District Council that meets incessantly.

' The province of this short paper, however, is not to praise ; it is to observe. And those who pore over this past period with historical eyes will delight to see how much each community has been learning from the other. There is the tacit admission that neither has the last word in town-building nor in citizen-making ; there is the knowledge, at long last, that each town possesses some-

thing that the other badly needs.  One beholds a peaceful pene-
tration going on, increasing in scope and value every year.  The
tradespeople in one town open shops in the other.  Ordinary
citizens pass and repass looking for bargains in one another's windows.  We take in one another's washing.  We copy one another's
ways.  You can see the old-fashioned Hitchin people being stung
into a new activity of life by the impact of a young and virile
community alive to its finger-tips ; insomuch that we, who were
once described as

> Drowsing the slow monotonous hours away
> In torpid ease,

are now very wide awake in our so-called Sleepy Hollow.

'On the other hand you can see the Modernists in Garden City,
who once upon a time proposed to found a Society for the Complete
Obliteration of the Past, satisfying their starved souls by visiting
the religious houses and time-hallowed haunts of Hitchin town and
by digging for Roman and British remains in their own astonishingly prolific soil.  It is ever so.  Dame Nature craves her balance,
and we half-cultivated people long for the things that will help
to make us whole.

'So the good work goes on.  We send our Hitchin architects
to restore the ancient and neglected parish churches of Letchworth
and Norton.  The Letchworthians send their architects to rid us
of our shameful wilderness of slums.  Nay, more : they make
Hermitage Road fit for us to shop in ; and they erect a luxurious
cinema for the improvement of our Quaker morals.

'In this mixing and intermixing some curious phenomena may
be observed.  It is, for example, an ironical commentary on English
industrial life that the strait-laced people of Hitchin should have
to send their sons and their daughters to Letchworth to make
corsets which Letchworth women obviously never wear, but which
their husbands sell at great profit to the less enlightened women
in other towns.

'The moral, or rather the immorality of that has been slowly
sinking into the consciousness of Hitchin people with the result
that, whereas aforetime we vowed that we would never sell our
birthright for a mess of factories, we are now proposing to follow
the better example of our neighbours and have factories without
the mess.

' I said just now that we at Hitchin were a strait-laced people. It would have been truer to say that we were so thirty years ago. There again we have learnt something from the vitality and independence of our neighbours. When I came to Hitchin in 1901, the town was still being brought up in the leading-strings of the Quakers. There was, no doubt, an advantage in their beneficent autocracy, for the Friends are acknowledged everywhere to be men of ripe judgment and organising power. The trouble was that no one else was given any hearing. The Quakers who never uttered a word were not disposed to listen to the words of others. It was a saying, still current, that not until you had lived for ninety years in Hitchin were you allowed to open your mouth. When that enlightened man Frederic Seebohm made his first speech at Hitchin, the aged Quaker minister, Samuel Allen, observed in his growl of a voice : " He is a young man to have an opinion."

' In Letchworth, on the other hand, the voice of public opinion has always had free course. It blows through their streets like a clean, vigorous wind from the east. From the very beginning there has been liberty, not to say licence, of speech for every citizen ; and for my part I think that in a multitude of opinions there is safety. Either nothing is done, or the best comes uppermost at last and is chosen to be done. In the early days of Garden City one had the impression of a thousand people all talking at once and at the top of their voices. It was dithering to our Hitchin ears. But it was, nevertheless, the sign of a hundred per cent citizenship and down with any dictator. Behind all that speaking, moreover, there was a good deal of hard thinking ; and seldom would it end with words.

' According to F. W. Rogers, before Letchworth was four years old, it had one committee for each inhabitant ; and from the majority of those committees there proceeded a volume of loud and wholesome protests against those who, for the time being, held the reins of office. I will not go so far as to say that Letchworth was governed by committee rule. But it owes much to what we might otherwise think to be the too-much protesting of its own citizens, and adds one more illustration of the truth of Horace Walpole's dictum, that the course of public virtue in this country is to be found in Petitions of Right and Grand Remonstrances.

' If these loud protestations had their direct effect in Letchworth

Garden City, they had an indirect effect, a repercussion, in the life of Hitchin. At certain periods in our long history we had found it beneficial to fall fast asleep; lulled, as our own poet George Chapman confessed, by those " prodigious securities in which we snore." But now, with the coming of Garden City, we sat up and took notice. First one and then another of our people took their lives in their hands and spoke, even from the house-tops, of grievances to be redressed, of old things to be made new, of town-planning, of road building, of slum clearing, of many other things. A new inflow of communal life resulted ; and with us, as with the pioneers of Letchworth, the modern world with its challenge, and its calls to social service, lay open to our view.

' And now for my fourth and last stage which, hardly as yet begun, is more a state of mind than any state of being. It seeks to find an answer to a pressing problem : " Where, if at all, do Hitchin and Letchworth meet ? " One school of thought there is which says, " They meet only to sunder." In their opinion it is better so. " Love your neighbour," said George Herbert, " but pull not down your hedge." They urge that each will do better work by offering its own distinctive contribution to the common stock. " It is better for the commerce of the spirit," I once heard Rabindranath Tagore declare, " that people, differently situated, should bring their different products into the market of humanity ; each of which is necessary and complementary to the others." There is much weight and wisdom in that view.

' Another school of thought there is which expects these two towns to meet, not in the flesh but in the spirit—in a higher synthesis. Out of the life experience of these oppositely-minded towns, they say, will spring a new vision of what each town in the future may attain. For this new race of practical-minded dreamers it is significant that, geographically speaking, Hitchin and Letchworth do meet—upon a hill. From their own still higher hill of vision they see the possibility of a " next time " Hitchin and a " next time " Letchworth, all gloriously built, within and without, with the common experience, harmoniously blending, of the old world and the new. After all, we are in our infancy as yet, and still have much to learn. In Hitchin we have built and unbuilt and rebuilt our town at least a dozen times. It may be the happy fate of Letchworth to have the same continuous chance of evolution. It may make a better use of it than we.

' The one thing needful, surely, is to go on building, urged by that same divine discontent I discerned in Ebenezer Howard. We have done something laudable already in our little day. We have emerged from being human into being humane; we have, as citizens of no mean cities, passed beyond being urban to become urbane. But let us not rest content with that. " This is not a world," I once heard a wise man say, " but rather the materials for a world " : and our poor human race, as it struggles blindly forward with its great and confused experiment of living, is never more worthily employed than in its striving to create the City Beautiful—the little counterpart on earth of the City of God. It is an attempt to express the inexpressible ; to capture what ever goes before and eludes the grasp of all our yearning hands. It is a mirage, I know, for the loveliest of our dreams have never yet come true. " This beauty's fair," said our great Hitchin poet :

> This beauty's fair is an enchantment made
> By nature's witchcraft, tempting men to buy
> With endless shows, what endlessly will fade,
> Yet promise chapmen all eternity.

' But the witchcraft lures us on and the difficulty of our task is but an incitement to proceed.

' Some parts of our task we have already achieved. We have repented of our ancient apathy and our feeling that as things have been so they will remain. " God has built a brave world," said our Hertfordshire worthy, Charles Lamb, " but methinks He has left His creatures to bustle in it how they may." That possibly is so. But, in the hundred years that have passed and gone since Lamb wrote those words, we have mapped and planned out our inheritance with almost scientific care, and are beginning to bustle in a less haphazard fashion.

' Other parts of our task are in the act of being achieved. And there again it is the mentality, the attitude that counts. We do not claim to be idealists, or " fellow citizens with the saints," but we are coming to see that towns do not live by ground rents or by trade alone, and still less by main-drainage and perpetual bureaucratic inspection. These things are not the life of towns, they are only aids to living.

' We are learning also that the mere agglomeration of people is not enough. There must be a pride of place, a local patriotism, a certain spirituality in town life. The mere binding of men and women together for some common purpose does not make their aim uplifting. If it did, then every joint-stock company would have a spiritual aim. Nor does it suffice to have all the towns-people thinking alike, drilled into uniformity of mind by the personality of one man or the dictates of an urban council. The Gadarene swine were unanimous ; but they all ran violently down a steep place and were drowned in the sea.

' Above all, we are coming to the conclusion that the planning and the building, the streets, the habitations and all that therein is, are only the outward and visible sign of something more worthy to be called a town. Do you not hear that cry out of Shakespeare's *Coriolanus* : " What is the city but the people ? Truly the people are the city." But there again the question must be pressed : " Who are the people ? " Are they Shakespeare's " fat and greasy citizens " ? Are they the merchants, the senators, the poets, the pilgrims of eternity passing through ? One thing is certain ; to have a fine city you must fill it with honourable men. Sodom and Gomorrah are believed to have been well planned ; yet ten righteous men were not to be found therein. Yes ; there are always plenty of people, but many a town has perished for lack of men.

' These are the questions that confront us in this our day and generation. Some of them, by the grace of God, or by our own counsels, we shall answer. It is sad that we ourselves should have here no continuing city. We shall leave much to be done by those who follow us. For my part, though I shall grieve to go from the light of the sun, and leave so many things unfinished, I shall feel that the future is in safer hands than ours. I think there will come a time, after we are dead and gone, when our children, wiser than their fathers, will learn to make an end of the insensate rivalries of territory and of trade ; will relegate those haughty adjectives Meum and Tuum to their proper subordinate place in the grammar of life ; and will contrive to build cities not only of bricks and mortar, but of flesh and blood, and with an indwelling spirit and a glory in the midst thereof.

' Then will come to pass that vision which the gentle Shakespeare beheld when, in his prophetic soul, he dreamed of things to come ; the vision of a " brotherhood of cities," the " unity and married calm of states." Then, and not till then, will it be possible to say that Hitchin and Letchworth meet.'

So far Reginald Hine.

Meanwhile as Sir Josiah Stamp says : " When you see a new idea don't throw half a brick at it. Search its pocket : there may be something in it."

# IX

# THE LAND QUESTION AT LETCHWORTH—I

*The result is to be more than a piece of skilful engineering, or satisfactory hygiene, or successful economics : it should be a social organism and a work of art.*

*Lascelles Abercrombie.*

IN the fun and movement of the early days Mr. Howard took a good-humoured part, but it is clear that his own interest lay in the land question. This was primary. How far could the public ownership of the land be maintained ? Could it be made to work as a practical scheme ? He knew that in many parts of the world eyes keener and more full of enquiry than any in North Hertfordshire were watching the Letchworth experiment.

Presently a division of opinion rose over an entirely concrete matter. The Directors of a Company wanted to buy a factory site in Letchworth. They insisted that the site must be freehold, and they did not want a site in the factory district, they wanted one of their own choosing.

All the land hitherto had been let on leases and the leasehold system was an essential part of the scheme for securing present control and the eventual increment of value for the whole community. The ideals of Letchworth were at stake. The factory was obviously desirable. It was a definite financial advantage to have it giving employment in the town and paying rates. Would the material benefit outweigh the Directors' loyalty to the scheme ? An animated discussion led to a full statement by Mr. Howard in the Magazine called *The City* which was then being ably edited by Henry Bryan Binns. The statement is characteristic in its painstaking assemblage of " pros " and " cons," its effort to deal with a concrete case on broad principles and its flashes of self-revelation. Reading between the lines it becomes a piece of self-portraiture and as such it deserves a chapter to itself. Here is a quandary. This book is meant to be read—not by experts who know all about the subject already—but by the plain man who knows only the facts and laws he runs across in the process of earning his living. A disquisition on land tenure is too heavy a strain to impose on the concentration of one whose attitude to all writers is : " If this man hasn't struck oil in five minutes he had better stop boring." Yet the phrase " land tenure " stands for something in the Garden City programme which it is vital to appreciate. The landlord as the mainstay of English agriculture has broken down under the burden of his own impecuniosity. He attributes his collapse to high taxation, though it has certainly had contributory causes for which he is partly responsible. If you enquire sympathetically what complaint the landlord died of, you will be told—in the words of a landlord's butler—" No complaints, sir ; everybody perfectly satisfied." There is therefore no question more urgent than that of finding some system to take the place of the old land-lord. Men and women have been driven off the land to make room for deer, pheasants, grouse and foxes. It is time to reverse the process. The country-side needs men and women as much as men and women need the country-side. There can be no settlement, no contentment, no settled family life till somehow the feudal ele-ment in the land system has been eliminated and a satisfactory co-operation has been established between the owner and the cultivator of the land.

Howard's contribution to the problem has not been sufficiently appreciated. Put briefly it is this. If the entire rights of the old landlords are vested in a public Company which holds the land in the interest of its tenants, and in which the tenants themselves hold shares, the tenant receives back in dividends a substantial part of what he pays in rent. Money paid in rent circulates but does not stagnate anywhere. It is the tenant's interest to cultivate as well as he can even if that means a higher rent—because a higher rent means a better dividend. Where landlord-control has become Company-control, exercised in the interest of cultivators, it ceases to be objectionable as control. Regulations can be observed, rules obeyed, rents paid, when they mean better organisation, better marketing facilities, better sanitation, better roads, better education. The tenant has become a member of a community and gets his share of everything that raises the standard of life in the community. The plan might be described as a practical method of subsidising agricul-ture without cost to the taxpayer or demoralisation of the cultivator.

LETCHWORTH—ON THE AGRICULTURAL BELT

Captain Reiss [1] summarises the arguments for the Garden City policy in *Town Theory and Practice* in the following paragraphs :

' There is great value in the whole of the land being in one ownership, because

' (a) It is then possible to prepare a comprehensive plan for the whole area.

' (b) In considering that plan, any reduction in the potential land value which may be brought about by restricting a particular area to agricultural purposes only, may be counterbalanced by the increases of value due to having restricted factory or residential areas.

' (c) The limitations in value due to land being used for open spaces or recreative purposes only may be balanced by the increases in value of the sites facing such land.

' In a word, the creation of land values will be in one hand. But it is not sufficient that the land should be in one ownership. The monopoly thus created must be used to public advantage. The predominating consideration in the preparation and carrying out of a town plan must be the interests of the town rather than the profit of individuals. Moreover, the excess of land values created over and above the amount required to cover the interest upon the capital cost of development must be used for the benefit of the town as a whole. These results can only be achieved by the whole of the fee-simple land not merely being in one ownership but in the ownership of some public body, whether Local Authority or the State, or else held by some person or body of persons in trust for the community.

' If this policy be adopted, then the following results can be achieved :

' (1) The main object of those preparing the town plan will be to secure the best possible town from the point of view of the citizens residing in it.

' (2) The same motive will inspire those responsible for the carrying out of the town plan, an operation which will, of necessity, take a considerable period of time, and will require continuity of purpose. However public-spirited a private owner may be, he cannot guarantee a like spirit on the part of his heirs.

[1] Captain Reiss in *Town Theory and Practice*, Chapter V.

' (3) In particular, the permanent maintenance of a belt of rural land can be secured.

' (4) Changes in land values created by the community will be enjoyed by the community.

' (5) Greater public spirit in civic life and a larger measure of co-operation for the public good by the general body of citizens will result from the sense of the corporate ownership of land and the consequent knowledge that improvements in value will go to public ends.

' (6) The grievances of the ordinary leaseholder on the renewal of the lease will be obviated.  Instead of the ground landlord for his own profit exacting the utmost farthing on such renewal, the fact that any additional rent does not swell private coffers will on the one hand be a restriction against extortion, and on the other ensure that the increase in value finds its way back to the general community.

' (7) The creation of vested interests is minimised, and thus one of the greatest obstacles to improvement is removed and greater speed and precision in development is secured.

' (8) Generally the corporate ownership of the land gives stability to the city.

' It will be seen that the garden city policy secures the main objects of those who advocate the taxation of land values and the nationalisation of the land, while at the same time it meets the objections of those who object to both proposals.  The fact that people holding widely divergent views upon the land question generally have agreed upon this policy, with regard to the creation of garden cities, is the strongest evidence of its soundness.'

With these broad principles in mind the reader may face Ebenezer Howard's lengthy exposition of land tenure in Garden Cities—or, if he prefers to do so, skip the rest of the sandwich and take only the jam in the middle.  But don't let anyone imagine that the dull details are unnecessary.  When an engineer is building a bridge he calculates the strain, then multiplies his figures by sixty. That is the " coefficient of safety."  Repetition of fundamental principles is the coefficient of safety in understanding and building Garden Cities.

LETCHWORTH—EASTCHEAP, CINEMA AND GARAGE

X

# THE LAND QUESTION AT LETCHWORTH—II

*From " The City," a monthly magazine now extinct.*

The answers frame themselves as the questions are analysed and explored.
*Lord Ashfield.*

ALL true progress in science and art is based upon observation, experience and experiment. We advance from practice to theory, and again from theory to practice. In social science—in the science of human relations—this is as true as it is in the science of chemistry. We must do, if we would know. We must act, if we would formulate true theories of action. And the almost inevitable result of new courses of action is the discovery of flaws in our theories, and these, if we are wise, we seek to remove, first in thought and then in more enlightened activity.

The essential aim of the Garden City as conceived in my mind was this : it was to unite people of good will, irrespective of creed or party, in a worthy purpose—the building of a city on juster, saner, healthier and more efficient lines than the cities of the old order. To this end I and those who worked with me sought to lay down a basis upon which common action could proceed, with as little danger of rupture and disintegration as might be. We soon found that all who were interested in the question were agreed in these propositions :

1. That there was terrible overcrowding in our great cities.

2. That our country-sides were rapidly becoming depopulated.

3. That it was therefore eminently desirable to attract people from places where they were in excess to places where they were insufficient in number.

4. That a combination of town and country life would be of great value.

5. That towns should be carefully planned and not allowed to grow up in a haphazard fashion, and that a very effective way of

69

proving this elementary but entirely neglected truth, would be to build a town which should be from the very outset carefully planned in the interests of its future inhabitants.

6. That as industries of various kinds frequently remove for purely economic reasons into the country and into small country towns, it would be desirable in the interest of the whole nation that a large estate should be purchased in an agricultural district and at an agricultural price, and special efforts made to attract industries to it.  That to this end special advantages should be offered to manufacturers and their employees—such as railway sidings, inexpenisve land (permitting of one-storey factories), cheap power, plenty of light, pure air, houses with good gardens attached, at rents low as compared with those of the crowded city, and in healthy surroundings near to the work and the play of the workers.

7. That it was also very essential to attract to the town a due proportion of professional and tradespeople and people of leisure, culture and refinement, and to attract to the agricultural zone (which it was deemed very important to provide permanently around the town), an agricultural population of whom a sufficient number should be provided with small holdings and allotments.

8. That as it could not be reasonably expected that any British Government would undertake such an experimental enterprise, it was necessary that those who believed in its value should unite and voluntarily subscribe the necessary funds, and create the necessary organisation.

9. That a Joint Stock Company, with limited liability, was the best and most practicable form for the organisation to assume at the outset.

10. That if the growth of the town was rapid, a large and rapid increment of land values would inevitably arise, and that such increment would afford a good basis of security for the capital invested.

11. That, in view of the public issues involved, investors should voluntarily, and in legal form, limit the dividends on their shares to some fixed percentage (afterwards settled definitely at 5 per cent), and that all profits after such fixed return should inure to the benefit of the community, either in the form of increased services or in the form of reduced rates.

12. That in due time the Company should be voluntarily wound

up, making way for a Trust representing the inhabitants, the share-holders receiving the par value of their shares, *plus* any accrued dividend not yet paid and a bonus of 10 per cent.

So far, as I have said, we found entire agreement as to our programme.

But, on the other hand, in regard to some very important details, considerable differences of opinion manifested themselves, and this at an early stage, and long before the Company actually got to work. Perhaps the most important of these differences was in regard to land tenure. At the outset I suggested the following system. (1) Perpetual leases, (2) Revaluation every seven years or so, when the rent payable under the lease would be raised or lowered, according to the increase or decrease in the value of the site, irrespective of buildings and improvements effected by the tenant. Now if this scheme had proved acceptable and work-able, the ultimate result would have been to secure the whole increment of land values to the people of the town, or to some Trust representing them, and would have created a fund out of which a large part of the public services of the community could be met. But this system did not prove acceptable, and therefore it was unworkable. There were, indeed, not a few who were so animated with a desire to make the project a very complete success, and were so convinced of the value and justice of the principle of the communal ownership of land, that they willingly agreed to leases of this kind. But many more, though personally willing to enter into this arrangement, found the way beset with difficulties. Their lawyers advised them against such a novel form of lease, warning them that they would not be able to dispose of it ; and, if they wanted to borrow money with which to build, the mort-gagees, or, if not the mortgagees, the mortgagees' solicitors, raised difficulties. And, I must confess, human nature, and especially custom, being what it is to-day, the difficulties were not by any means imaginary. Who was to undertake the task of valuing the sites every seven years ? How was the assessment to be reviewed if thought unfair ? Mr. A. might trust himself to be ready to pay a higher ground rent if his property improved in value ; but could he trust Messrs. C. and D. to do likewise ? Would not endless difficulties, jealousies and heart-burnings arise ?

Then it must be remembered that not a few helped forward this experiment even in the early days who did not at all hold this view

F

on the land question, and that very many of those who came
to Letchworth came (and we cordially welcomed them) simply
because they thought that Letchworth was an interesting and a
healthy place in which to live, or a desirable place in which to
conduct business.

Under these circumstances it clearly became necessary to modify
our proposals. For it is an essential principle implied in all con-
certed action of a large number of people that the rate of progress
must depend, not upon the speed with which the advanced guard
are ready to move, but upon the speed capacity of the rank and file.

The directors, therefore, decided to grant leases of ninety-nine
years at fixed rents—leases very much on ordinary lines. And
these leases give the Company and its successors the usual reversion
at the expiry of the lease to property erected upon the land. Now
this is a principle which, personally, I believe to be neither sound
nor just. On the other hand, the directors were in this grave
difficulty. To draw up leases departing too much from established
precedent would be to create all sorts of financial difficulties, and
these could not fail to affect adversely the tenants almost immediately. Besides, the leases would, of course, not expire for ninety-
nine years, and it is inconceivable that those who are then responsible
for the administration of the lessors' rights would be capable of
such an act of flagrant injustice as to appropriate without compensation all buildings erected on their land, or that the law of
this country would then permit such injustice, even if it were
contemplated.

But, in order to meet the wishes of those who are naturally
prejudiced against the leasehold system (as it has hitherto been
worked in this country), and who, therefore, desire longer leases
than ninety-nine years, the Company has granted leases on the
following terms. The rent fixed exceeds by 10 per cent the ordinary
rent, and at the end of the term of ninety-nine years the lessee has
the right to a fresh term of ninety-nine years at a rent to be determined by the then value of the land apart from buildings.

The problem which I will now endeavour to deal with, is, what
should be our future policy in the light of the experience we have
already gained ? I shall speak with that absolute frankness which
I believe is always best, but entirely on my own responsibility, and
for nobody but myself.

It is only by taking a somewhat comprehensive view of the

LETCHWORTH—THE BROADWAY

problem of city building that one can appreciate in its due pro-
portions the very difficult question before us, a question as to which
the sincerest well-wishers of the movement do undoubtedly take
diverse views.

The first point which may be fairly urged against the sale of freeholds at Letchworth is that this would certainly involve a change
of policy. The principle of the public ownership of land has been
a plank very generally accepted by supporters of the movement,
and embodied in many resolutions ; and it seems to me, therefore,
clear that no change of policy in this direction should be attempted
unless for the clearest and most cogent reasons. For nothing is
so harassing, nothing causes so much friction, nothing produces
such a sense of uncertainty and so damps enthusiasm—the chief
asset in all great movements—as a change of policy on broad and
clear issues. Indeed, even if a clear case is made out for such a
change of policy, some loss of enthusiasm is still inevitable ; while,
if such a case is not made out, then there is danger of atrophy and
even death.

The next point to notice is that our leasehold system has proved
successful ; for the growth of the town under it has been quite
phenomenal, especially when the difficulties inherent in a first
venture are taken into account. But, on the other hand, those
of us who are behind the scenes know that there has been in certain
quarters a demand for freeholds for factories (I shall here only
deal with the question of sale for such purposes), and it is suggested
by some that if such a demand were met it would lead to a more
rapid growth of the industrial elements of the town, to which we
all attach primary importance.

The question thus becomes somewhat complicated. On the
one hand one sees that the rapid growth of the town is essential
to the success of the scheme, and possibly even to the continued
existence of the town as a real Garden City ; but one sees, on the
other hand, that any effort to foster rapid growth which involves
a change of policy, may result in losses in other directions, difficult
indeed to measure, but, perhaps, far outweighing the apparent
gains of an easily-made concession. Who can value, as an element
making for healthy growth, an ever-increasing sense of unity of
purpose, more and more fully expressing itself in our ever-enlarging
social life, or measure the loss of power which comes from a breaking
up into rival camps, and a loss of this sense of unity ?   In one case,

every citizen is a missionary, compelling strangers to come in ; in the other, newcomers are greeted with less warmth. Public owner-ship of land makes distinctly for this unity ; it is, indeed, the embodiment of it, and, without that spirit, could not really continue to exist.

I think we can now conveniently consider the problem under several distinct heads.

First : How far would the sale of freeholds interfere with that measure of control by the community, which, if only it be wisely and temperately exercised, will prove to be for the benefit of all—a unifying influence, yet never hampering true individuality ?  I have had on this point the very kind assistance of a member of the Equity Bar, who has supplied me with the following statement of the law on this subject :

" There is one important difference between the freehold and leasehold systems as applied to the development of a building estate. This difference consists in the amount of legal control which the owner can retain over the user of the property in each case.  This control is effected by means of the covenants which the first purchaser or lessee of each plot enters into in his purchase deed or lease.  In the case of leaseholds, every covenant by the lessee, whether affirmative or negative, which concerns the land leased, can be enforced by the landlord and his assigns at any time during the term granted as against the first lessee and all assigns from him.  If the tenant commits a breach of any covenant in the lease (e.g. fails to repair the house or to keep the garden in order) the landlord may re-enter, and, unless the tenant remedies the breach, the lease will be determined.  The landlord can also re-enter as against a sub-lessee, although there is no contract subsisting between them.  The result is that the land is bound by the covenants during the subsistence of the lease, irrespective of the person who may occupy the position of landlord or tenant at any particular time.

" In the case of freeholds, all covenants by the purchaser can be enforced by the vendor against the purchaser and his estate after his death by an action for damages, and in some cases by injunction.  But affirmative covenants (e.g. to keep a garden in order) cannot be enforced against an assign of the purchaser. Negative covenants relating to the user of the plot (e.g. not to use the premises except as a private dwelling-house) can be enforced by the vendor against any person who may buy the plot with notice of the restriction. That is to say, the vendor can obtain an injunction in the Chancery Division to restrain the prohibited user. This right to obtain an injunction may be lost in various ways. For instance :

" (a) If a Garden City Co. permitted A, B, and C to open butchers' shops in a residential road, the Company could not obtain an injunction to restrain D from doing likewise.

" (b) If a Garden City Co. disposed of all the freehold of the city save the agricultural belt, and conveyed the belt to trustees for the community, the trustees could not enforce the covenants.

" (c) If the whole character of a district changes, it may become inequitable to enforce restrictive covenants.

" On the other hand, where there is a general building scheme for a particular area, the owner for the time being of any plot may have a right to obtain an injunction against the owner of another plot who infringes restrictions imposed on the whole area."

Without going into minutiæ, then, it is quite clear that the city, in parting with freeholds, would be parting with some measure of that beneficial control which it can retain in its leases ; and for this reason some elements of danger would come in, not the least of these being, possibly, an exaggerated sense of that danger.

The next point to consider is what would be the comparative results of the sale of freeholds, and the granting of leases.[1]

Let me put a concrete case : A and B occupy adjoining factory sites—sites of equal value. A has a ninety-nine years' lease, with right to a further lease at the end of the term, at a rent equal to the then value of the land, apart from buildings—such value to be fixed, of course, by an independent valuer. B has a freehold, for which he has paid £500. The Company is borrowing money at 4 per cent. In these circumstances, during the currency of the lease, unless there is a change in the rate of interest paid by the Company, or its successors, the financial results are the same in the case of the sale as in the case of the lease. But then it must not be forgotten that, if we are true City Builders, we are working not only for to-day or for to-morrow, we are working for generations

---

[1] For the purpose of this comparison I do not take into account the question of whether more land would be taken from the Company under one system than under the other, a point I shall touch upon later.

yet unborn ; and so we see that, while in the case of the lease the
(probably) greatly increased value of the land, apart from buildings,
would at the end of ninety-nine years revert to trustees for the
community, in the case of freehold the owner of the land and his
successors, who might be living in some quite distant place and
have no interest whatever in the Garden City, would be able to
enjoy the unearned increment.   Further, the owner of the factory
at the end of his ninety-nine years' lease would, as a rate-payer,
enjoy his full share in the increased rents paid on the falling in of
leases now being granted, provided he desired to take a fresh lease.

So stated, the question seems extremely simple, and an almost
irresistible argument seems to arise in favour of a retention of freeholds, but yet a closer examination will show that the question is
by no means so simple as it may appear.

Rapid growth, we all know, is vital to the success of our scheme.
It follows, therefore, that our land policy, whatever it is, must not
be too far ahead of the growth of public opinion.   Our policy may
be, *per se*, the wisest conceivable policy ; it may be a policy which
everyone will ultimately come to accept ; it may be a policy which
it will hurt us, as with a sharp blow, to give up ; but yet, if to-day
that policy is not understood and accepted by a sufficient number
of organisers of industry, and by a sufficient number of potential
shareholders and tenants, then the effort to preserve the policy
might mean that we not only fail on this important point, but on
many other points which are of, perhaps, equally vital importance,
and so the Garden City might degenerate into a mere building
speculation carried on primarily in the interests of its mortgagees.

I have purposely put the issue in this very bald way, because
I am sure it is the issue we have to face.   Are we strong enough,
wise enough, united enough, self-sacrificing enough, to maintain
our policy, and are there sufficient potential supporters and par-
ticipants in our movement whom we can draw in ?   Surely it is
worth a great effort, here at Garden City, to hold up the torch of
progress.

A great migratory movement of industries out of London is going
forward now.   Take a journey on the Great Western, and you
will see dozens of new factories being erected on freehold land.
These factories are dropped down, as it were, anyhow, regardless
of proper conditions of housing, of town planning, of social benefits
for the workers ; and no one with a seeing eye can fail to be con-

S. AND D. FREIGHTERS—OUTPUT OF A LETCHWORTH FACTORY

vinced that this unscientific, I might say this inhuman, way of dealing with the infinitely diverse problems of factory life, is, or soon will be, quite out of date. The flowing tide is not with but against this method of carrying on industry, and the freeholds which have been acquired by these factories represent, as I believe, a security not half so good as the leases of a Garden City.

This brings me to my last point. We must convince the manufacturer that our interests, and his, and the workers', are, at least on this point, one and undivided. He, quite rightly, must, before he comes, see in the Garden City, as those before him have seen, a sound business proposition. I would grant to every factory a long lease. I would not care if it were a lease of 999 years, subject to this, that the rent should be revisible at periods not exceeding ninety-nine years on the basis of the then value of the land apart from buildings, such value to be assessed by an independent valuer. And I would convince the manufacturer that it was to his interest to have such a lease rather than a freehold. You may say it would be difficult. But I would do it, or, at least, I would do it with the kind of man we most want, the man who would be a credit to our town, helping us so to build it that, when our structure was complete, it would be such a success, inwardly and outwardly, that its example would virtually put an end to a system of industry which regards a large reservoir of unemployed, and therefore degenerating labour, as one of the essentials of success.

I do not hesitate to say that I have had my doubts on this matter. I am, indeed, as my friends know, a man of some faith ; but I am also—perhaps the combination is somewhat rare—a terrible sceptic. Now, however, the measure of success we have attained, and the clear view I have of some of the main reasons why we have not succeeded better, and many other considerations I cannot here go into, have removed all doubts from our policy of retaining the freeholds for factories as well as for residences.'

# XI

## LETCHWORTH—AT INTERVALS OF TEN YEARS

A garden is a piece of common land, and yet it has ceased to be common land. It is an effort to regain Paradise.

*John Pulsford.*

ALTHOUGH it is still May roses are out, for summer has begun unusually early. Along Lytton Avenue the garden hedges are rich in colour and scent and as you pass along a whiff of sweet-briar comes floating across the side walk. On Icknield Way the almond trees are shedding their blossom, making the winding road look as if some fairy wand had transported it from the Riviera. On Norton Common the white May-blossom is throwing off the sweet heavy scent which pervades the air in all directions. The prairie —for Broadway is not yet laid out—is vocal with throbbing songs of larks tirelessly ascending and descending. Birds seem to know that they have right of sanctuary in Letchworth. Spring Road is getting its new yearly carpet of wild parsley which in that home of treasured loyalties which is called the New World goes by the name of " Queen Anne's lace."

An irregular thread of humanity in twos and threes is winding along across the Prairie, down Spring Road, past the old Letchworth Corner Post Office with its seventeenth-century brick and timber ripeness, down Letchworth Lane with banks like a Devonshire lane and overhead elm branches like cathedral arches. They are making for the Golf Links and soon there is a small crowd of about two hundred people on the sward by the Letchworth Hall Hotel. Although they have come to see Vardon and Braid play golf they cannot help feeling and talking about the beauty of the place—the Jacobean brick, the latticed windows, the piled roofs, the irregular courtyard, and the rich toned structure lying in its framework of green like a group of Allington pippins in a basket of green leaves.

The match begins and the crowd breaks up into groups to follow

Letchworth Hall Hotel and Golf Links.

LETCHWORTH HALL HOTEL AND GOLF LINKS

their favourite player, to watch the sinewy rhythm of Vardon's limbs or the muscular majesty of Braid's shoulders. For years the golfers who watched the match will tell and retell the story of Vardon's long flying parabolas, such as the stroke at the tenth hole that rose clear over the two trees two hundred yards away —not to be rivalled ever because the trees came down in a gale : or of Braid's miraculous luck too often thrown away on the green.

As the crowd dribbles back to the town discussing the game they find Letchworth *en fête* : May Day celebrations deferred for a month, in hope of getting a fine day, are in progress. A trades procession has been going through the streets. Children have been dancing in light summer dresses. Something is going on in the open space known as Howard Park. Follow the human drift and there, speaking from a small raised platform, is Ebenezer Howard. Two or three hundred people are listening curiously and with obvious pleasure as he tells once again the story of the great idea —how he had been made acutely miserable by the vile and verminous cabins in which people were living in London, in such districts as Somers Town and North St. Pancras, houses huddled round a yard that was a dustbin, with a single water-tap for half-a-dozen families—houses squalid, scabrous, verminous, smelling of disease and exhaling death. How under the stab of sympathetic pain he had dreamed his dream of transporting the victims of such an inhuman civilisation into conditions where they could live and work and thrive in such relations to earth and sky and air as nature intended for man. How the dream had taken form and shape in Letchworth with its essential fitness for human habitation. His hopes were now reaching out to a time when there would be many Letchworths and the rebuilding of the workers' quarters of London might begin.

### § TEN YEARS LATER. WAR TIME

The Great War did not leave Letchworth unscathed. Soon after the fall of Antwerp a diamond merchant from that city arrived in London with an offer to put down a quarter of a million in making munitions to get back at Germany. He found his way to Letchworth. A munition factory was about the last kind of factory Letchworth would have welcomed in normal times, but the necessity for shells was stern, pressing, and inexorable. So Messrs. Kryn

& Lahy, Metal Workers, built what was then the largest factory in Letchworth. Next came squads of skilled Belgian workmen smuggled over somehow with their wives and children. In a few weeks it was reported that there were three thousand Belgians in the town, who explained, " We are workmen, not refugees." They worked night and day in shifts of eight hours. All housing rules had to be suspended, beds were never unoccupied in houses where the Belgians lived. It was Box and Cox all day and all night. The shops were filled with sturdy, pushing women who wanted the best of everything, the best cuts of meat, the freshest butter, the newest eggs whatever the price. They must have beer, though Letchworth had no public-house. Quiet Letchworth residents not accustomed to shopping in a perpetual sale-scrimmage found it difficult to get served at all. The prices of houses went up and rooms were let and sub-let. For the time all rules were in abeyance.

Letchworth residents had not been brought up to take such abuses lying down and meetings were held. Ebenezer Howard would be on his feet half the time protesting against one thing or another which was ruining the fair fame of Letchworth. He had an ear for all grievances and the War was itself the worst grievance of all. It was a troubled, busy, crowded, anxious time for everyone, and at the best all a Letchworthian could hope to do was to survive till better days.

Then a new terror fell on the town. It was bombed from the air. The Germans had heard of the munition factory and sent over a Zeppelin to drop bombs on it. Fortunately the night when it arrived was foggy. The beating of the Zeppelin engine as it groped searching round the town was heard in every house. Then the bombs fell in pairs, one, two, three, a dozen explosions. The ground shook, the houses rocked, it seemed like the end of all things. Where had they fallen ? Who was hit ? Half the town was in the streets or gardens peering through the darkness for some sight of the enemy.

In the morning news spread that the bombs had fallen in the hundred acre field at Willian, killing one man who had been posted there to light flares for aeroplanes. He had lit a flare, mistaking the sound of the Zeppelin, and had drawn the bombs. The field was otherwise unoccupied and had provided a perfectly harmless target for the bombs.

When the next raid came and Letchworth was on tiptoe, suddenly the sky was lit up by a flare of light, and a streak of flame like a giant rocket came spinning through the air to the ground. The Zeppelin had been hit.[1]  A shout of relief rose from everywhere.  We could not see one another but we all saw the Zeppelin come down.  Quietly and in a subdued frame of mind people slipped off to bed.

Later the Germans made another attempt to reach the munition factory.  This time they scored a turnip field and the windows of some cottages nearby were broken by concussion.  Otherwise they did no harm.  But Letchworth became a darkened place for months. Regulations were strict as to lights, residents lived in the alcoves of their dining-rooms, and if a glimmer of light escaped a curtain they found themselves in the Hitchin Police Court.

Looking back on those hectic years it is fair to say that Letchworth came through them with credit though not without loss. Men of military age did their duty by their country in France, Italy, Mesopotamia, Salonika and on the seas, and some of them never came back.  The girls from all kinds of homes worked in the munition factories or in hospitals and earned a good report for mental and physical fitness.  They were practical, capable, mechanically-minded and efficient.  But no one in Letchworth would wish to go through that experience again.

## § TEN YEARS LATER

Great changes have taken place in Letchworth.  The cinder path across the prairie has disappeared and the Broadway with its avenue of Dutch limes and broad grass borders has taken its place. Substantial houses, standing each in its garden, line the broad road. The town square with its Lombardy poplars has been laid out as a public garden.  The cinema is filled twice nightly.  Attractive vistas open out as the roads take their permanent shape.  Norton Common has been fenced and green driftways run through it. Factories are increasing.  London coaches pass swiftly and silently through the town, linking the Garden City with the Metropolis. On the town football ground the local team scores miraculous goals to the confusion of its rivals.  In summer, cricket week draws its circle of spectators who watch as if the fate of Empires hung on

[1] This was the Zeppelin brought down at Cuffley.

the issue of the match. Houses are climbing the hill that looks
across the valley to the Chilterns. New roads are promising contact with the Great North Road and Bedford. There are schools
and churches in plenty. An arcade with attractive shops links
Leys Avenue with Station Road. The market gardens and holdings in Baldock Road are surprising the owners with their produce.
Motor-cars of all the rainbow hues come careering down Broadway,
some suggesting that Noah may have used them when it began
to rain and he was in a hurry to get into the ark, others that they
have just left a show window in Bond Street. Huge pantechnicons
indicate that the population of Letchworth is still increasing.
From five to six o'clock Baldock Road is one long procession of
bicycles, with twinkling lights as the evenings draw in, driven by
adventurous young people who make the best of both worlds by
living cheaply in some village home and earning Letchworth wages.
This is a modern industrial town. Not like anything else. Not
at all like industry in Lancashire or Yorkshire, Warwickshire or
Staffordshire. Still less like a country market town which sleeps
for six days a week to awake to feverish activity on one day in
seven. It is alive with the vitality of twentieth-century youth,
and is living by its own standards of health, vigour, intelligence
and sanity—standards which are making a good many typical
English things look out of date.

Of course there is a Rotary Club where the City fathers, carrying their success well in front of them, focus the interests and
discuss the future of the town which is their hobby and their pride.
To-night there is a special dinner in honour of Sir Ebenezer Howard
recently Knighted by His Majesty as a recognition of his public
services, and the Rotary Club, not to be behindhand where the
King has led, has made him an Honorary Member. We want to
see the social life of Letchworth so we shall brave the speeches.
The climax is reached when the short, bespectacled, bald-headed
man with blue benevolent eyes and a white military moustache
rises to reply to the toast in his honour. He explains that he has
been a Rotarian all his life, but never ventured to put his creed
into words till he found it done for him by Rotary. It is the only
creed that matters—Human service, honest friendship, friendship
through service, and service for friendship's sake, the success that
comes with frank loyalty to your ideals, the marvel of marvels
how a right idea once well worked out can penetrate the civilised

world and make new links to bind the world together.   A memorable evening, giving fresh heart to all disgruntled idealists ready to sacrifice their ideals for a small payment in cash.

> I will not cease from mental fight
> Nor let my sword sleep in my hand
> Till we have built Jerusalem
> In England's green and pleasant land.

# XII

## THE SPIRIT OF THE PLACE

The ancient Greeks and Romans were great civilised nations. Why? Because, besides governing and fighting, producing goods and selling them, they also produced spiritual things such as art and literature, and, what is far more important, they developed high types of humanity, and those great men are admired and prized by after generations. The chief end of civilisation is to produce men who, as we Chinese say, understand li-yo, courtesy, and music. A nation is civilised only when it has a spiritual asset or "realised ideals." The first thing you must do if you want to save civilisation is to know what civilisation is. Civilisation is first and above all a state of the mind and heart, a spiritual life.

   *Quoted from the Chinese by Lethaby, " Town Theory and Practice."*

PROFESSOR ARTHUR MARSHALL, the Cambridge economist, was one of the first of that "ilk"[1] to see that the old analytical political economy dealt with a state of society which was passing away because it had become obsolete. A new political economy was needed which had more of the Ten Commandments and less of the multiplication table. These are not his words, but they convey his idea. One of his addresses in which he predicted a migration from the great cities as a possibility of the future supplied a seed thought to Ebenezer Howard when he was formulating his own ideas.

Scientific political economy has never discussed whether it pays to work in squalor, ugliness, disease, disorder and dirt—whether industries which undermine health should be prohibited, whether health, beauty, order, cleanliness and scientific hygiene are important factors in industry, whether cities make the people, or the people make the cities. Marshall realised that political economy must be humanised, civilised, made constructive; but it was Ebenezer Howard who bridged the gulf and achieved the transition.

Letchworth folk often speak of the "Spirit of the place." But if you ask them what they mean by the phrase they will rarely give the true answer—which should be "the Spirit of Ebenezer

---

[1] Company, set or clan.

LYTTON AVENUE, LETCHWORTH

89

Howard." As a poet may write poetry better than his own explanation of it, so Howard let loose a humanising influence in civic economy which neither he nor any one else could have foreseen. A town is formed by spirit. A spirit good or evil—worthy or unworthy—is expressed in its whole conception and structure. The spirit expressed in the make-up of the town reacts on every one who lives in it. The repercussions are infinite and as varied as human personality. Any corporate society has something of the same moulding quality. There is one glory of Balliol and another of Merton—each turns out a different kind of man. One spirit of Trinity and another of John's. The types once set remain distinct to the end. The regiments of the British Army transmit traditions, customs, memories which form character, from one century to another, though the individual soldiers may be entirely changed. The regiment forms the men. The spirit of a town differs only in that it is more natural, more thorough, more permanent. In the United States where civic personality is more sharply defined because less diluted by outside influences, it is said : " New York asks of a man how much he has got ? Boston, how much does he know ? Philadelphia, who was his father ? Chicago, what can he do ? " Civic pride in these cities leads to endless and healthy rivalries.

" We have the finest cemetery in the United States," says the man from Philadelphia.

" Yep," says his neighbour from New York, " when I want a cemetery I'll go to Philadelphia."

" You have nothing like that in Chicago," says a rubber necker, pointing to a volcano.

" Naw, but we have a Fire Brigade that could put it out in ten minutes."

The man from Atlanta visiting Charleston under guidance of a resident admired the harbour.

" If we had a harbour like that in Atlanta we'd make Atlanta the second city in the United States."

" Waal, if you think so much of the harbour why don't you lay down a pipe line to Atlanta ? Then if you Atlanta men can suck as well as you can blow you might have the harbour ! ! "

Of course anything American is bigger and better and stronger and more absurd than anywhere else, but in reason civic pride is a good thing. It is good because it makes people different, it makes them take pleasure in different things. It makes them rival one another in having something worth talking about, if it is only a railway station, or a bridge or a factory or a park.

> We should build parks that students from afar
> Would choose to starve in, rather than go home,
> Fair little squares, with Phidian ornament,
> Food for the spirit, milk and honeycomb.[1]

Friendliness—freedom from class distinction—the " policy of the good neighbour," co-operation, public spirit, community service, a sense of fellowship with nature and all natural things have been characteristic of Letchworth from the beginning. They could hardly fail to be so in a town which had caught the attitude of Ebenezer Howard to his fellow citizens and to the outside world.

One conscious aim there is which is not commonly found elsewhere—balance. In this respect Letchworth is a more satisfactory medium to live in than any university town, manufacturing town, or residential suburb. A University town always has a surplus of intellect running to seed. A manufacturing town has no room for literature and it dislikes art as something foreign to its interests. A seaside town—which Germans call Vergnugungstadt—has to live for its visitors, it cannot be an end in itself. Our unbalanced towns are part of the price we have to pay for the sins of our forefathers.

There are many English towns which have achieved beauty but hardly one that would dare to say it aimed at beauty or balance. A thoroughly healthy community will recognise the right of every kind of occupation that makes for fuller and better life. It will encourage a balance of trade—machinery, sport and industry, manufacturing, agriculture, literature, music, art, drama, and if it is supremely wise it will recognise that civilisation cannot exist and develop without being rooted in religion, for religion is an essential factor in any organic conception of society. It would be too much to say that every Letchworth youth or maiden would own up to the effort to maintain such a composite balance, but it is true that this ideal is inherent in the foundation of the town and was actually in the mind of the founder.

If this were a history of Letchworth it would be right at this point to indicate how the success of Howard's plans was made

[1] Vachel Lindsay, "The Building of our City."

possible by the unselfish service and intelligent co-operation of a number of men more experienced than himself in dealing with the development of estates; the building of houses, the making of roads, and the management of Company finance. Some of these were Directors lending their capital and giving their time in a cause which they regarded as a constructive contribution to national well-being. Others were employees of the Estate Company whose zeal and ability were not measured by the financial remuneration they were receiving. Others were members of the Parish and Urban District Councils or officials who developed a gift for co-operation in the service of the common ideal, pouring oil on the new machinery when they might have wrecked it by throwing a monkey wrench into the works. The Founder of the Garden City sometimes quoted with approval a saying attributed to Andrew Carnegie: " I owe my success to the co-operation of men far abler than myself." His own share, he said, was like that of the person who pulls aside a curtain and opens a window to let the sunshine into a room. He doesn't make the sunshine, he only removes the obstruction which prevented it from doing its beneficent work.

The object of this study being not Letchworth but Ebenezer Howard and his share in a movement, it is relevant to note that an element of his success in keeping the movement going and carrying it to accomplishment was his frank recognition of the service of all his colleagues, his modest estimate of his own contribution, his willingness to accept the decision of others when he was outvoted in Committee, and his continual subordination of what might be regarded as his own interest to the success of the movement. Probably every colleague felt that he was a more important factor in the movement than Ebenezer Howard, and Ebenezer Howard was quite willing to let him think so.

## § REPLY TO A CRITIC

It may well be that our very survival as a civilised power and as a people may depend on how we now order the physical basis of our national life.
*Clough Williams Ellis.*

Thirty years after the publication of *Garden Cities of To-morrow* a captious critic has published a book, *Town and Countryside*, which deplores Ebenezer Howard's " muddled reasoning," " flabby thinking," and his mixture of " sociology and civics." Mr. Sharp's view is that Town Planning is an art, and as Ebenezer Howard was a reformer and not an artist his movement was a mistake.[1]

The obvious reply is that it is only Ebenezer Howard's work which has made Mr. Sharp's book possible. Criticism looks cheap when the critic is standing on the shoulders of the man whose work is criticised. It would have looked better if the critic had admitted that the experience which is the basis of his criticism could never have been gained if Howard's work had not been done first and done well.

But the substantial reply goes deeper. The reason why Howard was creatively potent and so many " civic artists " have failed was that he did look at his problem as a whole. It was exactly that mixture of " sociology and civics " of which Mr. Sharp complains. He saw that the long spell of industrial development in England had destroyed the natural adjustment of man to nature. That is fatal if it goes on long enough. " Civics and sociology " are pigeon-hole categories created by the human mind to enable it to analyse the total problem for purposes of study. They are no more. When we use them we are bound constantly to check their results by reminding ourselves that they are part of a total problem simple in essence though infinitely diversified in detail. The essential problem is a human problem—how men and women can live a good wholesome life as individuals, and as members of a social unit, under the conditions imposed by twentieth-century life. We cannot go back to the nineteenth or eighteenth century. We can only go on to the rest of the twentieth. We can complete our history, we cannot erase it.

Howard saw rightly that the only hope for the nation was to bring about a readjustment of man to nature, and it had to be man as he then was after a hundred years of industrialism. It had to be " man " with his industries, with the newest machinery, the best organisation, and the most recent discoveries of science, in order that the readjustment should not be, like Gandhi's efforts in India, a mere throwback into past history which, however sentimentally attractive, could never survive in the moving modern world. The readjustment was necessary not merely for æsthetic reasons, it was a question of physical survival. A doctor's account of the effect of town life as it was in the Victorian era on the human

[1] *Town and Countryside*, by Thomas Sharp. Oxford University Press.

TWO LETCHWORTH FACTORIES

constitution stated the case in this way : " The first generation which moves in from the country to the City does well. It has extra physical stamina, simple habits, and can outstay others in endurance of long hours and hard work. The next generation just about holds its own. It adopts city habits and the standards of urban or suburban mediocrity. The third generation is a martyr to all the ills that flesh is heir to. It has a struggle to keep alive and loses the ground financially and socially that the two earlier generations gained. As for the fourth generation, it ceases to exist. The family physique is worn out and seldom reaches maturity." Allowing for a sharpness of definition which ignores many exceptions there is enough truth in this statement to rouse serious alarm in the minds of people who think the English stock worth preserving. Mr. Sharp flings a gibe at these people—Lord Leverhulme, George Cadbury and the rest as " social reformers." They were keen observers of the facts of human life in their own time. They saw and dreaded the disease that was undermining the national stamina, they diagnosed it in the same way as did Howard, and they welcomed his specific treatment as the only one that seemed to " touch the spot."

After thirty years which have revolutionised the outlook of builders and buyers of houses, artists may see points where civic design might achieve more satisfying æsthetic results, but the motive power behind æsthetic criticism has no power to start a movement any more than a turning lathe has power to make a tree grow. Sound artistic work, and æsthetic perfection have their part to play even in the hygiene of town planning, for beauty is an ally of health and good temper ; they belong to the same family and help one another ; but no one ever succeeded in starting a movement in England which had nothing behind it but æsthetic principles. Mr. Sharp is more sure of his superiority to Ebenezer Howard than most of his readers. Even where he is right logically he is wrong biologically. Sheer beauty, says Abercrombie, is of singular *emptiness* in civic art. And *emptiness* is least desirable in houses. What is the use of beautiful and dignified crescents and squares if no one wants to live in them under present conditions ?

A sound appreciation of Howard's work must be based on a philosophy of human progress. The birth of an ideal means that the internal monitor is giving notice that he is not satisfied with the existing state of things. The protest is likely in initial stages to be sentimental in form and inadequate in expression but it is the first sign of new life. The ideal has a pull in it, a summons to create something better. The power to perfect the ideal comes later. The *métier* of those who see the ideal is to reject everything inconsistent with it, to avoid being led into culs-de-sac through which there is no progress. They must supply the motive power and leave it to others to perfect the machinery. This primary function in initiating progress Ebenezer Howard performed without a rival.

Mr. Sharp assumes dogmatically that the English are an urban race. There are many facts which would lead to a different conclusion. Certainly it is not true of the classes which regard themselves as typically English. For two hundred years it has been their custom to have " a house in town for the season," but with surprising unanimity they have agreed to spend as little time in it as good form would permit. A German observer with a keen eye has noted : " a peasant strain in the English character which comes out in all classes," [1] and this is right. Our leaders of fashion accept urban life as a duty demanded by their social position, but if anyone wants to see them when they are free to follow their own tastes and inclinations he will observe them " on the home farm," note their skill in breeding horses, cows, pigs, and sheep, shooting on Scottish or Yorkshire moors, fishing for trout or salmon, or hunting big game wherever it can be found. Some most characteristically English households are to be found in the Southern States of America—in Carolina and Virginia, where the domestic habits of eighteenth-century England have survived the shocks of political change. An abundant table is kept well supplied entirely by products of the home farm and surrounding coverts. Anywhere in the globe if you observe closely English habits are not urban. Even urbanity is difficult to maintain for any length of time. The difference between rich and poor is not a difference in character and tastes, but in the fact that the rich have the means to follow their instincts and the poor who would like to do the same lack the means.

Give the industrialised workman half a chance of keeping a few pigs, hens and a whippet or two, a kitchen garden and a few flowers and you will find how quickly the national character asserts itself. This is all to the good as an antidote to mechanised industry. It

[1] *Dibellius.*

tells on health, happiness, language, temperament, and makes a better man. Ask the men themselves and they will tell you that even the " diluted " country available in a Garden City is a long way better than none at all. Mr. Sharp's æsthetic principles are no doubt excellent and his style is good, but as a working proposition for men and women, children and similar animals Garden Cities have it every time.

It may be admitted as true that Mr. Howard's aims were human rather than æsthetic ; fortunately his advisers Messrs. Parker and Unwin had excellent taste and Howard had the good sense to accept their advice. He was not one of the people who thinks he has secured general agreement because he has done all the talking. He would have agreed that it was better to have large-minded people living in small houses than small-minded people living in large houses. The result in Letchworth is a town which has many claims to simple beauty, vistas which satisfy the æsthetic sense, houses that nestle into their surroundings, lanes that are a rural dream at all seasons of the year. Beauty is a pleasure almost akin to pain. Anyone sensitive to such thrills will sometimes stop, look, and listen, holding his breath at the sharp impact of some hitherto unrealised vista. One visitor returning to Letchworth writes :

No one returning after a lapse of years in which the building has pushed steadily towards its centre, and the roads lengthened out to its boundaries can fail to recognise the rare skill which planned and guided this growth. . . . Every fold in the ground, each ridge and hollow has been compelled to lend its aid to the general plan.[1]

There is a well-known class-type which uses the word " reformer " as a word of obloquy. It can hardly be spoken without a curl of the lip and a smile. We may give the word an entirely wholesome connotation when it is associated with Ebenezer Howard. A reformer is a man who feels the coming age acutely, by instinct and " in his bones." He tries to bring the minds of his contemporaries into harmony with the next stage in the evolution of human society. When he speaks of what he feels, with the conviction and assurance which it brings to him, he is regarded as one who dreams : so every reform passes through three stages. In the first it is impossible. In the next it is ridiculous, absurd. In the third " of course every one knew that it must be so, there is nothing remarkable about that." Howard had the unusual good fortune

[1] *Garden Cities and Town Planning Magazine,* May–June, 1928.

to see his reform pass through these stages and become generally, if not universally, accepted.　But that is no reason why we should forget that but for his existence—his character, his patience with his own impatience, and his persistence with other people's temperamental stolidity, his reform would still be among things regarded as impossible.

So much for Mr. Sharp.

# XIII

## WHERE GARDEN CITIES SCORE

What one really values . . . is a certain freshness, a startled and poignant apprehension of the beauty of the world, the spirit that calls so loudly in the ancient lyrical poetry of Greece and in our own Elizabethan poets.
*Times Literary Supplement, Dec. 22, 1905.*

THESE outline sketches of a Garden City are sufficient answer to the charge sometimes made that Letchworth is a " highbrow " proposition. When the epithet " crank " became no longer justifiable, " highbrow " took its place. It is not necessary to deny that there are some intelligent and thoughtful people in Letchworth, interested in art, religion, politics, literature, music, science, history, sociology and several other " ologies," and that they are there because it seemed to them the best use they could make of their lives. One of its own idealisms is that it may become a kind of popular university where young people can grow up with sound ideas of what a city should be—not from hearing lectures, but from seeing a few thousand people living a " good life." That may or may not be. The point is that regardless of " highbrows " there has been a vigorous social life taking all the usual forms : dances, dinners, concerts, camping, clubs innumerable, debates, card-parties, sewing-parties, receptions, public lectures, Scouts, Guides, athletic sports, flower shows and all forms of boy and girl self-expression. This strong social life is one of the main attractions of the Town and has borne out Mr. Howard's anticipation that the sense of a common civic interest would prove a unifying factor.

Meanwhile other events not contemplated by the founder have contributed to put the Garden City idea in the forefront of national development. In 1900 no one had foreseen the possible development of motor traffic. The founder thought of encouraging industry by laying down railway sidings. To-day any firm can have its own quick motor service daily, leaving Letchworth in the morning, visiting all parts of London, and returning in the evening. Trans-

99

port has become an additional Letchworth industry.  The vans
of London firms are constantly seen in the streets.

When Letchworth came into existence England was still the
" right little tight little island " it had been for a thousand years.
The experience of being bombed from the air in the Great War
and the assurance of a Cabinet Minister who had served on the
Committee of National Defence that " no power on earth can
prevent the bomber from getting through " has set people thinking
that the oldest argument for great cities—their superior safety in
war time—will have to be revised.  If England is to be liable to
air raids—and who can say it will not be so ?—then a Garden City
where houses and factories are spread over a wide area with plenty
of spare room is a much safer place than a great city—which offers
a perfect target for the bomber in a raid.  Improvements in the
supply of electricity—better telephones, the marvels of wireless
make it possible to be present at all important functions in London
without deserting one's own fireside.  Unforeseen changes such as
these have made garden cities more practical, more desirable, less
isolating, more in the main stream of human evolution.  The same
forces have operated in the opposite way in great cities—the congestion of traffic, the hoots of horns, the smells of motor exhausts,
the dangers of the streets, the rapid movements of population have
made London much less desirable as a place of residence.  Life is
more under control in a Garden City than in London.  Problems
can be isolated and dealt with, corporate civic life is more active.
More individual freedom and better organisation can be developed.
Fewer days are lost by ill-health and accidents.  Homes are nearer
to work.  Less time is lost in making necessary calls.  Business
can be transacted with promptness, efficiency and with less friction.
Circumstances over which the founder had no control have tended
to underline and underline again the soundness of his proposition.

Bombs may seem improbable but fires are among the risks which
have to be reckoned with.  Mr. Maurice E. Webb in an address
to the Royal Society of Arts reported in *The Times* of December
22nd, 1932, argues the case for town planning from the standpoint
of fire risk.   " London has become a vast conglomeration of buildings with no plan and no scheme, some twenty-five miles across.
From a fire point of view this uncontrolled building development
must be checked.  Factories and workshops, sometimes dealing
with highly inflammable materials, have been allowed to be dumped

down in residential districts without restriction, turning what was
a reasonable fire risk into a risk of high hazard for a whole street
or streets.

" Fire prevention is a definite function of town planning or town
and city reconstruction. Wide traffic arteries and more open
spaces are an absolute necessity to town planning from the traffic
point of view alone and they also diminish fire risks. At no time
in our history have such opportunities lain at our doors for modern
methods of construction, modern fire equipment, modern methods
of fire attack on one hand, and on the other a lay out of London
calling for a drastic readjustment to fit in with modern business
and traffic necessities."

The lines of pressure are converging—health, economics, sociology,
philosophy, business, agriculture, safety, convenience, athletics,
social advantages, all tend to meet in a form of civic organisation
which begins to look like the seed plot of twentieth-century civilisation. It will take time to win general recognition. A vast
amount of time and ingenuity will still be spent in trying to avoid
the consequences or remedy the effects of blunders which ought
never to have been made, to undo what never should have been
done at all. As this goes on the simple directness of Mr. Howard's
plan will commend itself to more and more people. It is easier to
start right and keep right, doing only what is consistent with the
end really desired, than to keep on patching a botched job. One
interesting evidence of success in a quarter where it seemed most
doubtful may be put on record. When *Garden Cities of To-morrow*
was published critics scoffed at the suggestion that anything could
be done to stem the tide of rural depopulation. It was inevitable
and must take its course. Since the war one Rural Council in the
Letchworth district has built 900 houses. This is not an isolated
case. Letchworth has turned the tide of population in North
Hertfordshire from an ebb to a flow.

Readers of these pages who have never been to Letchworth or
Welwyn will gather that Garden Cities have factories where industries are carried on—shops where " shopping " is not always a
burden, houses with verandahs and sleeping balconies, and cottages
with four rooms and kitchen, and an astonishingly low death-rate
almost negligible in the case of infants ; but it is possible to read
quite a lot about Garden Cities without realising that there are
gardens—real gardens—formal gardens—natural gardens—sunk

gardens—cottage gardens—factory gardens. The combined effect of these must be allowed to soak in before anyone can say that he knows all about Garden Cities. The writer once encountered a German Professor in Cambridge who professed to be deeply interested in Garden Cities. He took notes when I talked to him, and he asked many questions. At last I said : " If you will step into a car with me we can be in Letchworth in an hour, and you can go on by train to London after seeing the town. Won't you see it for yourself ? "

" No ! No ! I do not want to see anything. It is the theory I am interested in. I have got enough to tell my students in my lectures ! "

Lest anyone should fall into the dark pit of sightless theory let us try to picture some of the gardens in Garden Cities. If only twelve houses are built to an acre of land each of them has one twelfth of an acre for a garden, or they may be built round a circle or a square and throw their shares together in a bit of green sward, which is less trouble if you are not a gardener. But quite seventy per cent of humanity are children of Adam who, Shakespeare assures us, was a gardener, and also bore arms, for Adam digged and how could he dig without arms ? Consequently if you give the average man a bit of earth he will proceed to make it useful or beautiful. There is the garden at the Pumping Station which is a blaze of colour with red-hot pokers and salvia as you come into Letchworth on the Baldock Road. There is the Spirella garden, neat as a ladies' drawing-room, with bedding-out plants in season, a fountain in the middle and lots of odd corners filled in with saxifrages and Sedums from Gavin Jones' famous rock gardens. There are experimental seed gardens at the Country Gentlemen's Association, which at times make a brave show. In spring there are a hundred or two of gardens where you may experience what Wordsworth felt when he saw " a host of daffodils nodding in the breeze."

> And then my heart with pleasure fills
> And dances with the daffodils.

In the house built by Mr. Hugh Dent when he lived in Letchworth there is a round bed of flaming Darwin tulips bordered by forget-me-nots which, when you have seen it once, you will look for every year. There is the Coppice with its lovely rose garden hidden from observation, from the Hitchin Road, by the tall pines in the

LETCHWORTH LANE—TO THE GOLF LINKS

little wood that gives its name to the house ; and elsewhere a host of exotic shrubs from many parts of the world, one planted by Ebenezer Howard himself.  And " Glaedhame " with its lovely patches of purple aubretia and yellow violas—its lily pond and velvet lawn, and " Corriewood " looking for all the world as if it had walked out of *Country Life* with its grass paths and its sundial. There are roads in Letchworth where every house has a rose garden, for roses grow in Letchworth clay as freely as gorse on a common. The town garden which lies four-square inside a belt of Lombardy poplars is a botanical garden and a flower show all summer.  You can go there and learn the names and scents of new plants for your own herbaceous border.  Letchworth came into existence just at the right time for herbaceous borders.  Miss Jekyll had published her evangel which shattered the gardeners' idea of the garden as a place which ought to be made to look like a drawing-room carpet. She had opened the gates of a garden of Eden where behind borders of arabis and forget-me-nots, irises, and lupins, campanulas, montbretia, sweet sultan, verbena, gladiolus, dahlias, sweet peas, Michaelmas daisies, anchusas and pæonies, anemones and phloxes, delphiniums and chrysanthemums may in their season vie with one another in friendly rivalry as to which can get most sunshine.[1]

One lady gardener who was sent to the United States to study garden architecture and afterwards visited Letchworth reported that she had seen nothing so interesting in horticulture as she found in Hertfordshire Garden Cities.

Cynical people in London have said that garden citizens had more gardens than they knew what to do with, and some have spoken of them as a burden.  But these are town folk who have not yet discovered that a garden is a sacrament of beauty, and beauty is one of those draughts of the divine which give spiritual peace, evenness of temper and new courage for the work of life. Living face to face with Nature makes it difficult to be discouraged. Even when she disappoints us she comes back to make it up with an extra largess.  It makes one healthy to live in a garden, in mind as well as body, so that you can't sit down and brood over your neighbours' sins or the worries, resentments, vexations and bitterness that come from living in a crowd.  How can you help

---

[1] These varieties occur in a herbaceous border twenty-two yards long and averaging three yards in depth.

being happy if you are healthy and in the place you want to be ?

> Not God ! in gardens !  When the eve is cool ?
> Nay, but I have a sign ;
> 'Tis very sure God walks in mine.

If it is a function of religion to bring a man to himself, to keep him sane, and quiet and serene, a garden is a place of sound learning and true religion.   One could fancy sometimes that in these abodes of silent thoughtfulness fellow-working with nature, gentle hands of blessing are laid on one's head.

The largest public garden in Letchworth is Norton Common, seventy acres of old time common land covered with blackthorn and hawthorn bushes and other trees which the Garden City Company had the good fortune to inherit.   At all seasons of the year it is tenanted by flocks of birds, the rise and fall of whose chatter when they gather for migration can be heard all over North Letchworth.   The gardens that look on to the Common on both sides have a double harvest of the eye for their owners.   Norton Way which leads to old Norton village has many charming gardens.

Flowers are the scenic product of these gardens but there are others not less beautiful and more permanent.   Apples grow as abundantly as roses, and in a good season Letchworth Bramleys, Allington Pippins and Grieves can hardly be beaten.   Here the Red Coat Grieve was born and started on its career.   The apple orchards are a sight to rest the eyes when the blossom is on the trees.   Few gardens are without them and the small holdings in Baldock Road carry wonderful crops in a good season.   Kitchen gardens are not so beautiful to look at, but when the annual show comes round the exhibits indicate that the gardens are making their contribution to good house-keeping.   No peas, beans, potatoes, sprouts, cauliflowers or strawberries are ever so full of vitamins and flavour as those grown in a man's own garden, planted by his own hand and cultivated with an enthusiastic spade : so it may be put on record that Garden City is also a city of gardens.   As you compass the boundaries of this Zion anyone may feel that

> He is nearer to God in a garden
> Than anywhere else on earth.

There is so much scepticism about the possibility of transforming an agricultural belt from a liability into an asset that it is important to let the smallholder speak for himself.   The following letter is

LETCHWORTH—GARDEN ORCHARD AND PASTURE

106

from W. G. Furmston who is well known in Letchworth as mine host of the People's House—the public-house without alcoholic drinks. The letter was written to *John Bull* in response to an account of " Bill Smith who could not keep from singing now he was back on the land." It is eloquent as first-hand testimony from a man to whom Letchworth has meant life, independence, health for himself and his family and a competence. Note that the £3,000 which has been paid in wages is money made on the orchard—it means that the writer has put back what he received for one year's fruit harvest into the orchard in labour, seeds, manures and the like for the next year. Meanwhile he and his family of eight have had the produce of the orchard as a contribution to housekeeping. In his own words " even in years when the accounts show a money loss there is a net gain in terms of life." For pioneers from choice or necessity this letter is the challenge of a genuine rough diamond.

111, BALDOCK ROAD,
LETCHWORTH,
HERTS,
*June* 18 30.

DEAR JOHN BULL,

Not all Bill Smiths can sing, but many more can get back to the land and do as Ruskin said, if they would. Thirty years ago I was in a London factory, artificial light most of the time, and wife in rooms with children. It worried me what would happen if I got out of work. We determined to emigrate ; went on the *Ruapehu*, a New Zealand ship, saw the accommodation, and were preparing to go. Got stock of clothes, needles and cottons, tools, woodman's axe, and what we thought might be wanted. Then came the Garden City movement, and instead of leaving all friends and relatives, we built a cottage here for £300, and rented $2\frac{1}{4}$ acres of land.

I got other occupation here after 3 years, always kept at work as we had to borrow money for house, etc. Others who could dig or prune or the hundred and one jobs there are to do, have been employed at various times to help, the income being too small to develop, and knowledge and aptitude on my own part not enough, never having had a garden before.

The result is that on this ground some £3,000 have been spent in wages in 25 years, about £1,000 in seeds, manure, ground rent (there is no ownership of land other than secure lease from First Garden City), greenhouse, bees, ducks, fowls, trees, plants, bushes, stringbaskets, and all kinds of things, nearly all of which has been got back in produce.

As I write a string of people are going up to buy plants, it having rained, and we always buy best seeds, Sutton's, as Vincent the Brighton waiter used to recommend. Others as well like Unwin for peas, Bunyard for nuts and black currants.

I enclose some recent pictures taken by Julian Taylor while the apples were in bloom.

If there is any point of interest that could be enlarged, would gladly do so.

I can't sing—was turned out of every singing class I went in, and that was many, up to 30 years old—but have been able to show how to bring a family of eight children up, and keep a bit of old England cultivated as it should be.

We can hear the blackbird, thrush and cuckoo, gather a cherry or a strawberry, apple or nut, blackberry or flower and say to the flying motorists scurrying past on the Hitchin-Cambridge road, "You are going nowhere better."

With best wishes,<br>
I remain, Yours sincerely,<br>
W. G. Furmston.

P.S. This article was written while at home this afternoon after reading *John Bull*.

We have sought not to make a business, i.e. take other's, but to cultivate a piece of England thinking England should grow her own food and that here is the cure for our troubles,—Housing, Employment, Safety. Dependence for food on other countries is dangerous ; the submarines sank food last time. Next time it may never leave the other shores.

# XIV

# WORDS AND FACTS: GARDEN CITIES OF TO-DAY

Beware of substituting verbal for real solutions of the problem.
*Dr. John Watson.*

SOME super-intelligent person has remarked that definitions would be valuable if words were not used in making them. Any one who has tried to make an ideal clear by definition knows the perplexity created when the words of his definition have to be re-defined by other wordy definitions. That is why an ideal can hardly be communicated at all and certainly not felt to be attractive until people see how it works. A definition to touch reality must include both words and facts. The definition of a Garden City worked out by the experts of the Garden City Association is as good as words can make it:

" A Garden City is a town designed for healthy living and industry, of a size which makes possible a full measure of social life, but not larger: surrounded by a rural belt: the whole of the land being in public ownership or held in trust for the community."

Yet it has taken thirty years of strenuous work to make clear what this definition means, and the meaning is so full of satisfactory content that it required a skilled hand like that of Sir Edgar Bonham Carter to set it out in detail for a Parliamentary Committee. It required twenty-six printed foolscap pages to explain what Sir Edgar now means by a Garden City—too much for reproduction but a perfect mine for quotation. As there are many points on which the public is still misinformed and many that it has never " taken in," some extracts from the evidence of the Chairman of the First Garden City for Lord Marley's Committee are entirely relevant to the purpose of this book.

The present Letchworth Estate comprises some 4,562 acres, that is to say, some seven square miles. Its length from north to south is over four miles and its breadth from east to west about three miles.

Before a sod was cut or a brick laid the Directors proceeded to have a plan prepared of the future town. The Town Plan was prepared by Messrs. R. Barry Parker and Raymond Unwin (now Sir Raymond Unwin). It contemplated an eventual population of from 30,000 persons and divided the Estate into a central town area comprising about 1,500 acres and a surrounding agricultural belt. The main principles underlying the Plan are simple and convincing. The land is put to the use for which it is best suited, separate areas being allocated for factories, for shops, for a civic centre and for residences.

The area for factories was laid out along the railway, where there was level ground suitable for factory buildings and sidings, and is about 135 acres in extent. The site has other advantages; it is screened by rising ground from the rest of the town, and being at the north-east of the town, the prevailing winds carry any smoke away from the town. Most of the factories employ electricity for their power, so that little smoke is produced. A secondary small factory area of about ten acres, not provided for in the original Plan, has been developed to the west of the railway station on the north of the railway line for light industries not needing railway sidings, and a further area has been earmarked for factories.

The main shopping and commercial centre is situated in the streets in proximity to the railway station. A few subsidiary shopping areas are permitted at specially selected points in the residential areas to meet the convenience of residents.

The Town Square, situated on high and level ground in the centre of the Estate, is reserved for a civic centre. The Museum and Secondary School are there, and sites have been reserved for the Town Hall and for Churches.

The rest of the town is residential. The cottage estates were first grouped in convenient proximity to the works. When that area was filled, cottage estates were located on the western edge of the town area, to the south of the railway, and a cottage estate is now being built towards the western boundary of the town area on the north of the railway. The last-mentioned estate is the most remote from the works. The distance from its centre to the centre of the works is about one mile and a quarter only. Many parts of the Estate provide attractive building sites for more important

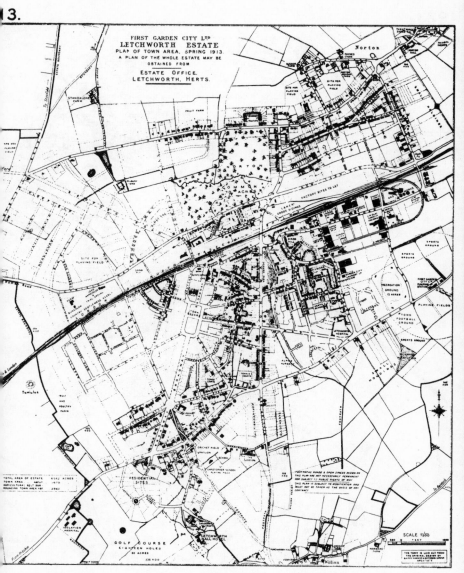

FIRST GARDEN CITY LTD
**LETCHWORTH ESTATE**
PLAN OF TOWN AREA, SPRING 1913.
A PLAN OF THE WHOLE ESTATE MAY BE
OBTAINED FROM
**ESTATE OFFICE.**
LETCHWORTH, HERTS.

# DEVELOPMENT MAP OF LETCHWORTH GARDEN CITY.

## 1923.

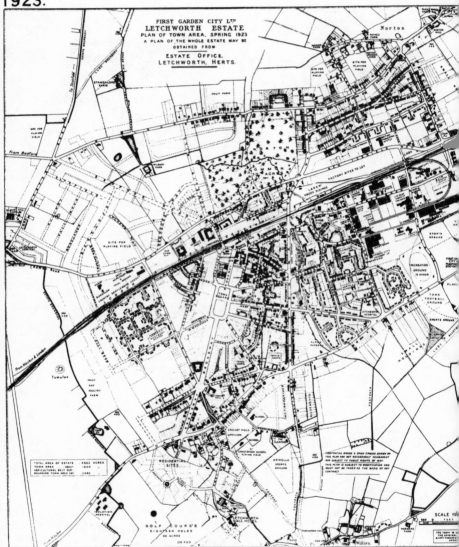

FIRST GARDEN CITY Lᵀᴰ
LETCHWORTH ESTATE
PLAN OF TOWN AREA, SPRING 1923
A PLAN OF THE WHOLE ESTATE MAY BE
OBTAINED FROM
ESTATE OFFICE.
LETCHWORTH, HERTS.

# Development Map of Letchworth Garden City.

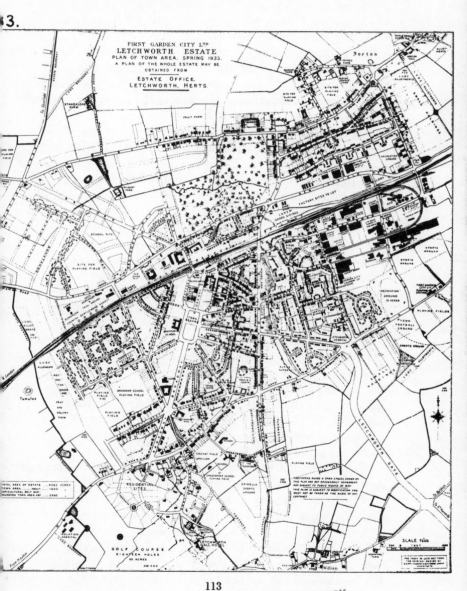

FIRST GARDEN CITY LTD
**LETCHWORTH ESTATE**
PLAN OF TOWN AREA, SPRING 1933.
A PLAN OF THE WHOLE ESTATE MAY BE
OBTAINED FROM
ESTATE OFFICE.
LETCHWORTH, HERTS.

residences, but perhaps the situation most sought after is the south-west corner in proximity to the Golf Course, Letchworth Lane and Sollershott. The lay-out is spacious. The maximum density permitted is twelve cottages to the acre, and over the greater part of the Estate a much more open development is provided. Every residence stands in its own garden.

The roads were planned and laid out with a view to carrying the eventual traffic of the town. Though motor transport at the time when the Plan was made was in its infancy and few could have foreseen its growth, the planning of the roads has, with minor exceptions, stood the test of time. The two main roads giving access from the Hitchin-Baldock Road to the centre of the town are Broadway—a fine boulevard 100 feet wide, with a 24-foot metalled carriageway—and Norton Way, which is 60 feet wide and has a 16-foot carriageway along part and 24 foot along the remainder. Access towards Bedford will be provided by the new Bedford Road, which is 78 feet wide with a 24-foot carriageway and is being gradually constructed as the town extends. Subsidiary roads are mostly 40 feet wide with 16-foot carriageway. Most of the roads are lined with grass verges and are planted with trees.

The increase of motor traffic and especially of heavy motor lorries from the Factory Area created a need for an improved means of access to the Great North Road. This has recently been provided by a new road 150 feet wide with a 30-foot carriageway connecting the Hitchin-Baldock Road, at its junction with Pixmore Avenue and Pixmore Way, with the Great North Road. The new road was constructed by the Hertfordshire County Council with the assistance of contributions from the Ministry of Transport, the Letchworth Urban District Council and First Garden City Ltd. The land for the road was given by First Garden City Ltd.

Generous provision has been made for recreation grounds and sports fields, of which further particulars are given.

Surrounding the whole town is a belt of agricultural land comprising about 3,000 acres. This acts as a protection from overgrowth from within or without, and assures that the country-side shall always be within walking distance of the centre of the town.

Some forty acres are let as allotments.

The planning of the town has been carried out by the First Garden City Company by means of its powers as sole owner of the Estate, and not by the Local Authority under the powers of

the Town Planning Acts. The Urban District Council has, however, a voice in the Town Plan. To ensure this, the Company has
deposited with the Council a " lay-out " plan of the town, together
with an explanatory memorandum defining user, character of buildings, and density, etc., and has agreed not to depart from the
provisions of the plan without first consulting the Council. This
would enable the Council, in the event of their objecting to the
proposed changes and failing to come to an agreement with the
Company, to pass a resolution under the Town-Planning Act to
prepare a Statutory Town Plan. The result would be to prevent
the Company from modifying the provisions of the Plan unless
authorised to do so as the result of the inquiry by the Ministry of
Health.

It has not been the policy of the Company to build itself, although
in special cases it has done so either directly or through subsidiary
Building Companies. The method adopted in the development of
the Estate is for the Company to provide roads, water, drainage
and other public services, to lay out the plots and to lease them.

Generally speaking the practice has been, and is, for the Company to construct the roads, and lay the sewers. The Urban
District Council takes over the maintenance of the roads when
they are completed, provided they are made up to their specification.

On the purchase of the Estate it was surveyed for water and
for drainage. Almost the whole of the Town Area can be drained
by gravitation.

To start with, the Company undertook the drainage and the
sewage was disposed of on temporary sites by means of broad
irrigation. The Company recovered the cost from Lessees of property connected to the sewers, who, under the terms of their leases,
were required to pay a special charge for the purpose. In 1922
the Urban District Council took over the sewers and the work of
sewage disposal, and in 1923 they constructed permanent sewage
works at a cost of £57,166 on the site on the extreme northern
boundary of the Estate, which, as the result of the original survey,
had been reserved for the purpose.

The number of villas and residences amounts to about 1,420.
Most of them have been built by individuals for their own occupation, or as an investment, or by local builders for sale. A few
have been built by a Building Company. The Company has not
built villas itself, with a few exceptions, and no large scheme of

villa building has been undertaken.   The cost of the great majority
of the villas erected since the War has varied between £600 to
£1,500.   The cost of a few has exceeded £2,000.   To finance the
building or purchase of their houses a large number of persons have
borrowed from the Urban District Council under the provisions of
the Small Dwellings Acquisition Act, or from Building Societies.

By a special arrangement with a Building Society the Company
has guaranteed an advance to approved purchasers of small property in excess of the normal advance made by Building Societies.
By this arrangement purchasers have obtained 90 per cent of the
purchase price, repayable to the Building Society over a term  of
years.

One of the principal objects with which Letchworth was founded
was to provide better housing conditions for working people than
could be found in the old towns ;  and much thought and care was
given by the Company and others in the early days to providing
attractive and healthy cottages of a good standard at the lowest
possible cost, which should be within the means of the workers
in the town.   The experience gained at Letchworth before the War
did much to raise the standard of cottage building throughout
the country, and has had an important influence on the type and
character of the cottages provided since the War under  municipal
schemes.

The great majority of the cottages erected before the War were
built by Public Utility Societies.   Their capital was obtained partly
by shares and loan capital, the dividends on which were limited,
and partly by loans from the Public Works Loans Board.

Since the War the Public Utility Societies have not been able
to continue building, except on a very small scale, since they have
not been able to raise their capital on such favourable terms as
the Urban District Council, and the work has fallen to that body.

The rents charged, including rates, are as follows : For a cottage
with a living-room and three bedrooms, 8s. 11d. to 9s. 3d. ; and
for a cottage with a living-room, parlour and three bedrooms,
10s. to 14s. 6d.   Only a few cottages were built in Letchworth
before the War by the Hitchin Rural Council.   Since the War,
the Letchworth Urban District Council has been very active in
cottage building.   There can be few, if any, Local Authorities with
comparable resources who have built so many cottages.

Letchworth has good reason to be proud of its cottages.   I know of no industrial town which provides better housing or better conditions as to health and amenity for the working-classes than Letchworth. The Urban District Council has performed an admirable piece of work in cottage building. But it should not be overlooked that the Council was greatly assisted immediately after the War by the special provisions of the Addison Act. Under that Act it was able to provide the large number of 707 cottages at the cost to the town of 1$d$. rate only. Even so, at times since the War there has been a shortage of cottage accommodation, and it seems clear that if a rapid industrial development were to take place the Council could not meet the demand for cottages except by raising the rates to an amount which would be injurious to the future development of the town. Additional facilities are, therefore, required to meet the possibility of increased demands for cottage building.

Areas leased to various clubs and sports organisations amount in all to over 160 acres. These include the Golf Club, the Town Cricket Club, the Town Football Club, and the Town Tennis Club. Many of the factories have their own sports clubs and sports fields.

Recreation Grounds held by the Company amount to about five acres.

The rents charged by the Company for playing-fields are, generally speaking, much below what would be charged in an ordinary town.

Though the growth of the town has not been so rapid as its founders anticipated, Letchworth has grown into a thriving residential and industrial town and is steadily increasing.

A single paragraph from the evidence submitted by the Garden Cities and Town Planning Association helps to complete the picture :

" As Letchworth and Welwyn have proved, Hertfordshire provides an eminently suitable field for enterprise in the founding of garden cities or satellite towns. It is near London, and has excellent communication with it by road, by rail and by canal. Easy access to London is one of the chief requirements for the success of a new industrial town, for although there is a tendency towards the decentralisation of industry, there is, on the contrary, no likelihood that the chief industrialists themselves will move from their offices in the City. There is another reason for encouraging industrial communities in the area round London rather than elsewhere, for by doing so those industries which would otherwise find sites in the Metropolitan Area may be located outside, to the relief of congestion and to the general benefit of the community. It is clear that in choosing a site for a satellite town the needs of industry must first be considered, because if the location is not attractive to industrialists no industries will be founded there and the scheme will prove abortive from the outset. Good communications are essential by railway, by road or by canal; cheap electric power and an ample water supply should also be provided. In addition, there should be plenty of land available for extension and near the industrial area there must be a healthy and attractive site for housing those the industries employ.

" When a new town is planned beforehand, it is quite possible to avoid most, or even all, the disadvantages usually associated with industrial development, and to make a place that is attractive to the eye and healthy to live in."

If anyone wants to know what a Garden City means it is safe to refer him to Sir Edgar's evidence. If statistics are wanted they are there. If finance, it is also there in sufficient detail to satisfy all but the incorrigibly curious. But even then it is better to live in Letchworth for at least six months, say from April to October, if you wish to be quite sure of the meaning of the facts and figures. When you have fulfilled this condition you will not require Parliamentary evidence or statistics; you will know for yourself that Sir Ebenezer Howard was right—sanely, surely, simply, satisfactorily right.

# XV

# WELWYN GARDEN CITY

## STATUTORY RECOGNITION AND STATE ASSISTANCE

I should like to see a political economy beginning with this idea, not how to gain the greatest wealth, but how to make the noblest race of men.

*Benjamin Jowett.*

THE year 1919 marked the second stage of the Garden City movement, but Howard's idea of a second garden city at Welwyn goes back earlier than 1919. Between 1912 and 1918 he told me many times—writes Mr. Osborn—that he had his eye on an ideal site for the second scheme. ' In 1918, before the end of the War, he insisted on taking Purdom and me to walk over it. We went one Sunday by train from London to Hatfield, and walked by way of Hatfield Hyde right up to the present centre of the Welwyn Garden City Estate ; and he convinced us that the site was suitable enough to be noted in case we were challenged when lecturing (as we often were) to show that possible sites existed. We even prepared a rough sketch at that date showing where the new town could be placed—purely a theoretical speculation in connexion with our lectures and the writing of *New Towns after the War*, in which Howard was directly and personally interested.

' It was entirely a coincidence that the greater part of this land came into the market at the Panshanger Sale in May 1919. Howard, I think, saw in this coincidence the finger of destiny. At any rate he became for the time being a different man. Ordinarily rather amenable and plastic, when the possibility of his second scheme appeared to him to arise, he ignored, defied or derided the advice of all his friends, including the immediate circle of enthusiasts who were trying to revive the propaganda of garden cities on a large scale, and went right ahead, on his own responsibility, to buy the land. The more cautious, if not more realistic, minds of all his colleagues in the Garden Cities Association and New Towns Com-

WELWYN—SHOPS AND OFFICES, HOWARDSGATE

*Howard Memorial in Foreground*

mittee, were dead against any more garden cities being started by
private enterprise ; they were concentrating on getting garden
cities fused into the great national housing schemes then being
discussed.   Howard's attitude, then and always, was :
'"If you wait for the State nothing will be done.   We must act
ourselves.   If you won't act, I will."
'And he did.   By sheer force of personality and enthusiasm he
obtained from a group of friends (notably Mr. J. R. Farquharson,
Mr. Franklin Thomasson, Mr. H. B. Harris, Mr. G. Blane, Capt.
R. L. Reiss, Lt.-Colonel—now Sir Francis—Fremantle, M.P., and
Dr. R. O. Moon) enough money to pay the deposit on the purchase
of a group of the Panshanger farms.'

Welwyn was one of the beauty spots of Hertfordshire, the land
was well wooded, there was sand and gravel in places, a stream
borders the estate, the site was only twenty miles from London and
there was a railway station already on the north end of the estate.

Mr. Howard's own account of what happened on the day of the
sale was :

"I knew that the reserve price was to be £30,000, and a few
days before the sale I had only £1,000 in sight.   That had been
promised if I made a second effort to build a Garden City.   I got
busy on the telephone and by ten o'clock I had another £2,000
promised, two offers of £500 and one of a thousand.   That was
10 per cent on the purchase price, enough to pay the deposit.   So
I went to the sale, made my bid and secured the site of the second
Garden City."

The following letters give Mr. Howard's own recollection of the
Welwyn purchase and record the high hope he entertained for the
new venture.

5, Guessens Road,<br>
Welwyn Garden City, Herts.<br>
January 10th, 1927.

My dear Farquharson,

Many thanks for your very encouraging letter received this
morning.

In the matter of this "honour" there would have been comparatively little to go upon had not you and I had that conversation in the Board Room of First Garden City when you agreed
to make your contribution two thousand pounds and not one

thousand only—a fact which helped me there and then to get one thousand from Thomasson and a loan to myself of five hundred pounds from Harris, repaid out of moneys afterwards raised, and later in the day a further five hundred from Blane.

Even then it was a close shave, and, as you know, Saville put up two hundred pounds or so of his own money in the Auction Room.

You and I are, I am sure, convinced that there was a beneficent Power behind us.

Yours very truly,
(*Sgd.*) EBENEZER HOWARD.

*To Mr. Langston of " Langston's Patch."*

HOMESGARTH,
SOLLERSHOTT R.,
LETCHWORTH.
*June* 1919.

DEAR LANGSTON,

I have just been able to seize a unique opportunity of acquiring what I have for some time been convinced is one of the best possible sites for a second garden city in the neighbourhood of London. Part of the site has just come into the market, and, after taking expert advice, which more than confirms my own opinion, I have, with the help of a few friends, paid a ten per cent deposit on 1,450 acres of land on extremely favourable terms. The remainder of the necessary land, I have good reason to believe, can be obtained at a fair price from an adjoining owner who is in real sympathy with the garden city movement.

The position is almost ideal from the point of view of providing for some of the industrial and housing needs of the London region. It is twenty-one miles out from London on the Great Northern Railway main line and at the junction of two branch lines connecting with the Midland and Great Eastern Railways, and there are excellent factory sites. Road access is also good. Gravel, brick-earth and chalk are plentiful, the lie of the land lends itself remarkably to inexpensive development and there is no difficulty about water.

On certain parts of the estate building could begin at once, and much of the property is extremely beautiful.

As soon as possible a Company will be formed to develop the

WELWYN STORES

estate as a garden city, that is, a complete town with its own industries, power-plant, public services and so on, surrounded by a permanent rural belt. Steps to this end must be taken with the utmost possible energy in order to obtain full advantage of the present Government Housing Scheme.

(*Sgd.*) EBENEZER HOWARD.

About the time when this crucial step was being taken, Mr. Howard—not yet Sir Ebenezer—was the guest of the present writer at Bramble Bank, Letchworth. We were going together to a dinner, and half an hour before we were to start he came downstairs saying that he had no dress tie. Not having any in the house, Mrs. Macfadyen sent to our neighbours, Mr. and Mrs. Barry Parker, to borrow the desired article. Mrs. Parker sent two—one of her husband's and one of her son's—so that Mr. Howard might have a choice. When he emerged to go to dinner he had *both* ties on. He had evidently concluded that this was a new fashion which he had not encountered before.

Additional land was afterwards secured, rounding off the site, making it about four miles in extent. A pioneer Company was formed as in the former case and capital raised. Sir Theodore Chambers—a valuer of wide experience and much authority— adopted the scheme and became the prime mover in the construction of the new town.

The times were difficult. Money was scarce and dear, and in its early stages Welwyn Garden City had to raise money at high rates. Against that it was able to make some economies in road-making, laying drains, and general development, benefiting by experiments which had been costly in Letchworth. On the other hand, Welwyn was determined to make its own experiments.

One which was very near to Mr. Howard's heart was, in the early days of the scheme, to have one general Store where all household necessities could be bought. All other shops were prohibited for a period of 10 years. This experiment was only partially successful, because " Selfridges " don't grow on every bush, and none of the Welwyn bushes have produced one. The Welwyn Stores remain, but other shops are being admitted gradually as the Town grows. Experiment has not yet discovered the exact middle way between the plethora of small competing shops, which must in the nature of things die off, and a single Store which offers obvious advantages and economies, but necessarily comes under fire from a public accustomed to a variety of shops and reluctant to surrender the apparent benefits of competition.

The growth of Welwyn was phenomenal. It was particularly successful in attracting factories which are a familiar feature of the landscape to travellers on the London and North Eastern Railway. The short distance from London made it convenient as a "dormitory town" and its proximity to the Great North Road made it familiar to motorists.

Many people had recognised that the next stage in the Garden City Movement must bring in Government action in some form. Questions were being asked in the House of Commons. Letchworth and Welwyn were getting into perorations of important speeches, and people were asking, "What is the Government going to do about it?" What actually happened was that Garden Cities made an unobtrusive entrance into Parliamentary life in Mr. Neville Chamberlain's Unhealthy Areas Committee Report in 1920. Opposites suggest each other—and the Committee opined that Garden Cities were better than slums and might be recommended as a cure for abominations standing where they ought not. In July 1921 legislation was passed to enable the State to assist the development of Garden Cities schemes approved by the Ministry of Health. Welwyn was first in making an application under the new Act, and was the first Association authorised to receive a loan from the Public Works Loan Commissioners.

The Garden City Movement might be described in the modern scientific terms as a movement proceeding on the method of trial and error. In a changing world it assumes that experiments must be made. Each new Garden City adds something to the common stock—each learns something from the experience of others. Features common to Letchworth and Welwyn require no emphasis, but in some important respects Welwyn has made departures from the Letchworth plan of operations. These new features are described in the report prepared by Welwyn Directors for Lord Marley's Committee and may be summarised here:

The Company set out to build a town of a definite size (about forty to fifty thousand inhabitants). With this end in view the area of land to be acquired was carefully considered. The reasons, among others, for its suitability were:

Being about twenty miles north of King's Cross, it was near to, but definitely separated from, London. The Great North Road skirted it on the west side. The main Great Northern Line bisected it and two branch lines radiated east and west from the main line about the centre point of the estate. Its general character was suitable for urban development.

By a coincidence two-thirds of the present site was put up for auction by Lord Desborough, together with other outlying portions of the Panshanger Estate. Sir (then Mr.) Ebenezer Howard, with the financial backing of a few individuals, purchased this portion at the auction. The remaining third of the land necessary in order to complete the site was the property of Lord Salisbury, who agreed to sell it at a similar price to that paid for Lord Desborough's land. The total acreage obtained was about 2,400, at an average price of about £50 per acre.

It is necessary to give the reasons which have led the directors to build up a network of subsidiary undertakings for carrying out various classes of work in connexion with development, a policy which is in marked contrast to that adopted by the First Garden City Limited at Letchworth. It was the definite policy of the Letchworth Company to confine itself, so far as practicable, to land development and the provision of the main public services.

At Welwyn the policy of the directors has been to undertake any subsidiary enterprise if it seemed desirable for the purpose of stimulating general development. As to whether they would have adopted this different policy if times had been normal and prices static, is difficult to say. Certain of the directors were of opinion that, quite apart from the special difficulties of the time, it was desirable to carry out subsidiary enterprises as a means of utilising to the full the advantages of the Company's ownership of the freehold.

However this may be, the special difficulties in the early days, caused by the dislocation of the post-war period, led the directors as a whole to adopt the present method of organisation, as will be explained later.[1]

In broad terms, the policy pursued by the Company has been as follows :

Welwyn Garden City Limited (the Parent Company) has, with

---

[1] *Note by Captain Reiss.*—Sir Ebenezer Howard's view was that in the special circumstances of post-war years subsidiaries were necessary. But he was not one of those who took a strong view that subsidiaries *in any case* were desirable.

some trifling exceptions, confined its direct operations to the purchase and development of the land itself and the construction and administration of the Sewage Disposal Works and the Water Supply. These latter two undertakings have been transferred during the present year to the Urban District Council. All other operations (with some minor exceptions), which the Parent Company thought it necessary to undertake, have been conducted through subsidiary or associated organisations, registered either under the Companies Act or under the Industrial and Provident Societies Acts. The capital required for these has been found partly by the Parent Company, in the form of investments and loans, and partly direct from outside sources, such capital being, however, for the most part raised for them by the Parent Company. The subsidiary and associated undertakings at present in existence are as follow :

Welwyn Garden City Electricity Company Limited ; Welwyn Public Utility Society Limited ; Handside Houses Limited (own houses for letting) ; Welwyn Builders Limited (carry out building contracts and jobbing work) ; Welwyn Stores (1929) Limited. Retail trade (bakery, dairy, coal yard, etc.) ; Herts Gravel and Brick Works Limited (production of sand, gravel and bricks) ; Welwyn Transport Limited (owns and operates light railway system and horse transport ; also a pit for the production of road stone) ; Welwyn Commercial Buildings Limited (owns and lets industrial and commercial property) ; Playhouses Limited (owns the Cinema-Theatre) ; Digswell Nurseries Limited (nursery gardens, landscape gardening, maintenance of playing fields, fruit farm, etc.) ; New Town Trust Limited (owns certain properties of a special kind) ; Welwyn Publications Limited (owns the local weekly newspaper).

All the foregoing are trading undertakings, and the controlling, and in most cases the entire interest, in them is held by the Parent Company. In addition, the Company held the controlling interest in Welwyn Restaurants Limited (a company owning or managing licensed premises), but has recently sold the predominant interest and now only holds a quarter of the shares.

There are also two subsidiary organisations which are purely Holding Companies, namely : Howardsgate Investment Trust Limited and Welwyn Garden City Investments Limited. The existence of these is due to adventitious circumstances connected with the problems of development.

The Directorate has varied in members and personnel from time

WELWYN—A RESIDENCE COURT

to time. Broadly speaking, there have been about eight or nine
Directors appointed by the Shareholders, together with three Civic
Directors [1] appointed annually by the Local Authority. Of the
Shareholders' Directors, four have usually been resident in the
town. Practically all of the Directors have been concerned with
other businesses as well as that of Welwyn Garden City. Three
of the resident Directors, in addition to attending the Board and
Committee Meetings, have been and are now concerned with day
to day direction. It has definitely been found better in practice,
however, not to appoint a Managing Director. The three local
Directors giving continuous supervision to the Company's work
do not carry out direct executive management, but supervision
and co-ordination. They meet constantly with the Heads of
Departments of the Parent Company and the Managers of the
Subsidiaries, and are available for consultation. These three
Directors do not give their whole time, and it has been thought
better, as a result of experience, to have three part-time Directors
rather than one full-time Managing Director. The Board of the
Parent Company meets as a whole once a month. In addition,
all the Directors—other than the Civic Directors—serve on one or
more of three Committees or groups, the three local Directors
referred to above serving on all such Committees. These Groups
are :

(1) Deals with the general purposes of the Parent Company and
acts as the Board of the following subsidiaries : Welwyn Garden
City Electricity Supply Co., Ltd., Welwyn Public Utility Society
Ltd., Welwyn Commercial Buildings Ltd.

(2) Deals with the business of Welwyn Builders Ltd., Herts
Gravel and Brick Works Ltd., Welwyn Transport Ltd.

(3) Deals with Welwyn Stores Ltd., New Town Trust Ltd.,
Digswell Nurseries Ltd., Playhouses Ltd.

All these Committees make reports periodically to the main
Board and all important matters are referred to the main Board
for their decision. In addition to the foregoing there is a Finance
Committee which meets periodically to consider financial matters
and makes an annual review of the Company's expenditure, including salaries.

Three of the Directors serve on the Board of Welwyn Publica-

---

[1] *Note by Captain Reiss.*—Civic Directors is another difference from Letchworth.
Sir Ebenezer Howard was responsible for this innovation.

tions Ltd. and one represents the Company on the Board of Welwyn Restaurants Ltd.

The principal Officers or " Heads of Departments " of the Parent Company are :

The Secretary and General Estate Manager, Financial Secretary and Chief Accountant, Engineer, Surveyor and Estate Agent, Property Manager, Two Architects, and Staff and Welfare Manager.

The subsidiaries each have their own manager and staff, but certain functions, chiefly accountancy and secretarial, are carried out by the staff of the Parent Company for the subsidiaries, and the cost of this is charged out to them, as also is a portion of the Directors' fees and remuneration.

It should be pointed out that, apart from ordinary business-management and direction, the local Directors and principal officers of the staff give a considerable amount of their time, of necessity, to matters which, whilst not strictly connected with the actual business of the Company, are, nevertheless, closely associated with it. A large amount of the social services would not have come into existence but for the activities of those first connected with the Company. Constant problems arise in connexion with such matters as the development of health services, hospital and social amenities and recreation, which require a considerable amount of attention from Directors and Staff in order to ensure smooth working. It should be emphasised that though this work is not directly connected with the Company's business yet, if it were not undertaken, the Company's business would undoubtedly suffer.

When the Company issued its first Prospectus in 1920, the market rate of interest was exceptionally high. Gilt-edged securities were standing at a low figure and yields of well over 5 per cent could be obtained by investments in British Government Securities. Publicly advertised prospectuses of well-known and established companies offered high rates of interest. Welwyn Garden City Limited's Prospectus offered Ordinary Shares with dividend limited to 7 per cent and with no certainty that such dividend would be earned. Not unnaturally the amount actually subscribed totalled less than £100,000. The necessary extra amount of capital required for the purchase of the land and for the early development was found by loans from the Company's bankers, personally guaranteed by the Directors. Later 6 per cent Debentures were issued, but

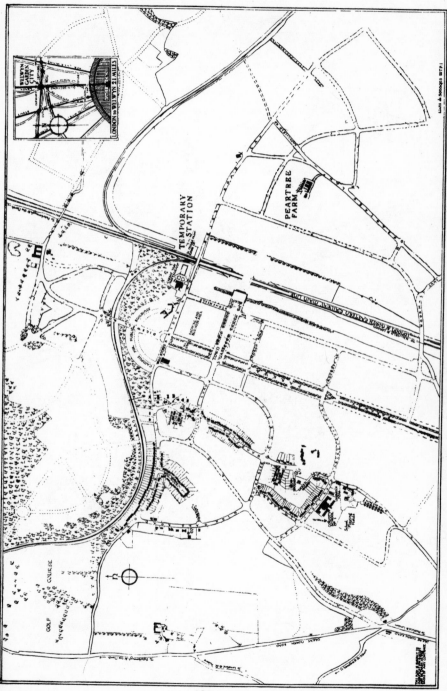

PEARTREE FARM

TEMPORARY STATION

GOLF COURSE

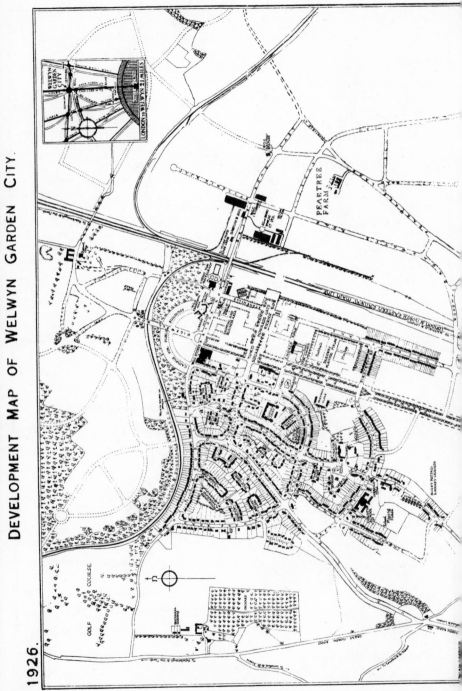

DEVELOPMENT MAP OF WELWYN GARDEN CITY.

1926.

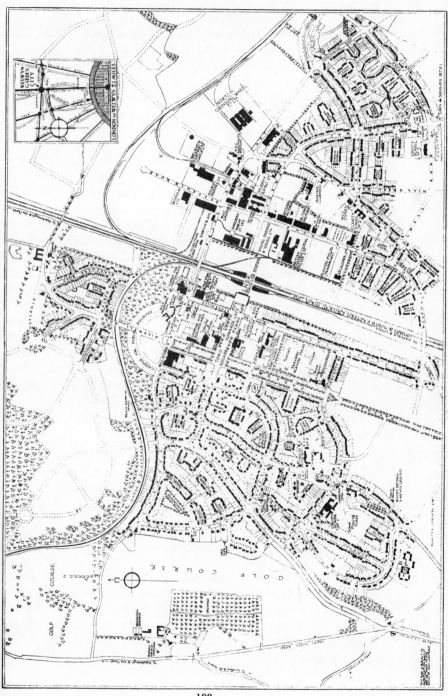

the capital from the public only came in slowly and did not keep pace with the necessary capital expenditure.

In 1921, partly as the result of the report of the Departmental Committee on Unhealthy Areas, presided over by Mr. Neville Chamberlain, Parliament included in the Housing Act of 1921 a clause permitting the Public Works Loan Board to make loans to " Authorised Associations " established for the purpose of developing Garden Cities.

Welwyn Garden City was the first body to become an Authorised Association under the Act, and immediate steps were taken to apply for a loan from the Public Works Loan Board. No other body has, in fact, obtained loans under the Act.

It should be pointed out that the Public Works Loan Board act under the general powers given them by the Public Works Loan Act of 1875. This Act requires the Board to have regard to the security offered and gives them discretion as to the amount which they may lend under any special power given under any Act of Parliament. It is of vital importance to bear this in mind in considering the question of whether the Public Works Loan Board was the best machinery which could be devised if Parliament wished to further the establishment of Garden Cities.

In granting loans the Board exercised their general powers, but were limited by Treasury regulations as to making loans to Authorised Associations establishing Garden Cities.

The regulations issued by the Treasury provided, *inter alia*, that :

(a) The loan should not exceed three-quarters of the value at any time of the security (i.e. in the case of Welwyn Garden City—the Estate and the Water Undertaking).

(b) The loan should not exceed an amount equal to the sum raised from other sources.

(c) The loan should be advanced for the purpose of development approved by the Ministry of Health.

In 1922 the Company obtained its first loan from the Board. From time to time thereafter the Board advanced further sums. These loans were at varying rates of interest and provided for repayments by equal half-yearly instalments covering interest and principal, the periods of the loans varying from twenty-five to thirty years.

The fact that the Company was able to obtain these loans in the early days undoubtedly saved the situation, as there was extreme difficulty in obtaining a loan at reasonable rates of interest from other sources. It was soon realised, however, both by the Company and by the Public Works Loan Board, that the machinery established by the Act of 1921 was really unsuited to its purpose. The Public Works Loan Board have always had grave misgivings as to the granting of these loans, and, on the other hand, the Company was subjected to certain restrictions in the way in which the loans were made, the terms of repayment, and the necessity of having to work in close relationship with a body which really was not anxious to lend at all.

The provision of houses, factories, shops, restaurants and other buildings does not in itself make a town; certainly not the community life envisaged by Sir Ebenezer Howard.

Provision has to be made for all kinds of social services: for the establishment of public halls, churches, etc., and above all for the knitting together of the community in such a way as to secure for it the best possible use of the advantages which the environment affords.

The Herts County Council and the District Council have both exercised, so far as it was reasonable to expect, having regard to the circumstances of the time, the various powers which they possess for providing social and health services.

The County Council has built elementary schools, though there has been some disappointment that they have not yet constructed a secondary school, and have exercised their power of making grants towards the Child Welfare, and other health services, since that duty was transferred to them from the Ministry of Health. Acknowledgment should also be made of the great help afforded by the Medical Department of the Ministry.

The District Council has taken its part in the maintenance of the verges, street trees, and small open spaces which have been taken over by them from time to time. They have also acquired an area for playing fields. They have made a grant from the rates towards the maintenance of the Public Library and have, in various ways, made good use of the powers they possess.

The activities of these public bodies has, however, required a large amount of supplementing by the Company and by various voluntary associations which have been established in the town.

K

WELWYN THEATRE : EXTERIOR

In 1921 a group of residents were got together to hear an address from Lord Dawson of Penn, and, arising out of his suggestions, the Health Association was formed. This association has two main committees : one dealing with hospital treatment, and the other with maternity, child welfare and district nursing.

A small cottage hospital has been established and arrangements made with other hospitals to take cases which cannot be dealt with in the local institution. Substantial sums of money have been raised for the maintenance of this hospital and towards its original cost, but the extent of the hospital provision has naturally been limited by the difficulties of raising money.

The other committee has established an excellent service by the provision of two Infant Welfare Clinics, one on each side of the Main Line, which are hèld weekly, together with two Ante-natal Clinics. Until recently this committee was also responsible for the running of Dental Clinics in connexion with the schools, but this work has now been taken over by the County Council. They also provide for District and Maternity Nursing and employ a Health Visitor and School Nurses. In all, four fully trained nurses are now employed. Grants towards this work are obtained from the Herts County Council and the Herts County Nursing Association, but a large amount of the cost is borne by voluntary subscription and the Company has contributed liberally towards the work.

About the same time as the Health Association was formed, the Educational Association was brought into being. This body owns three different halls in the town which are used for social and educational purposes. It provides for adult education and has raised considerable sums to provide additional equipment in the County Council elementary schools. It was also responsible for starting the Free Library, which now has its own committee and receives certain grants from the Urban District Council, but raises considerable sums of money every year to supplement this provision.

In addition to these two Associations, there is a local Guild of Help, a branch of the St. John Ambulance Brigade, and various other bodies of a similar nature.

In 1927 a " Central Civic Fund " was established for the purpose of assisting to raise money for those organisations dealing with the social services in the town which were of a non-partisan and non-sectarian character. The committee of this fund has consisted of representatives of the various participating bodies and of the business community and trade unions.

In addition to collecting subscriptions from individuals, this Committee has established an "Industrial Scheme" under which a large proportion of the business houses and factories contribute 4*d*. per employee—2*d*. by the employer and 2*d*. by the employee. In return, the employees who are in the scheme obtain for themselves and their families free hospital treatment and various benefits from the other organisations covered by the scheme.

The Parent Company and all its subsidiaries contribute under this scheme.

Various religious communities have constructed their own buildings. There are two new ecclesiastical parishes which now have parish halls for use as churches and are raising money for the building of their permanent churches. The various Free Churches have combined to construct their own building on the west side of the line. They have built also a small church on the east side, and soon hope to construct their permanent building there. The Roman Catholics have built a Church and Convent School in Parkway.

The Society of Friends and Gospel Mission have their own meeting houses and certain other religious bodies hire public halls for their services.

It is now twelve years since the first brick was laid in Welwyn Garden City. During those twelve years a purely agricultural estate, with five farm-houses, labourers' cottages and one mansion house, has been transformed into a town of 9,000 inhabitants with 2,500 houses, and some forty industries; with shops, theatre, schools, churches, banks, playing fields, macadam roads; with a complete drainage and water supply, electricity and gas. It may fairly be said that there is a town in being and that the objects of the enterprise have been substantially realised.

It may be claimed also that there is beauty in the architecture, the streets and the public gardens, and that the health and social life of the community has reached a standard far higher than most small towns can boast, and without the evils which large urban agglomerations bring in their train.

It is an essential feature of garden city development on its economic side that a large amount of capital expenditure has to be incurred well in advance of possible revenue-earning capacity.

WELWYN THEATRE : INTERIOR

It has always been recognised that, in the early years of such development, a considerable amount of interest on borrowed capital will have to be added to capital which will accumulate at compound interest during a period of time.

The experience of Welwyn Garden City Limited has shown that, granted reasonably static conditions with regard to costs and normal and reasonably static rates of interest on borrowed monies, the establishment and development of a garden city is definitely an economic proposition. But we suggest that the establishment of garden cities is too large an operation to be carried out, except as a pioneering experiment by enthusiasts, without the assistance of the State or some public authority. This was recognised by Parliament in the Act of 1921, but the machinery set up thereby has proved unsuited to its purpose.

The long period which must elapse before the full fructification of the scheme means that a comparatively small amount of capital can be obtained at reasonable rates of interest, and that chiefly from people actuated by public, as opposed to purely private, considerations.

If, therefore, the Committee is of opinion that the establishment of such garden cities is in the public interest, we suggest that some public machinery must be set up which will provide a substantial amount of the loans necessary, at any rate in the early days of development, and that the body actually responsible for making the loans should be definitely instructed by Parliament that the object is to establish garden cities. Whilst being cautious as to the scheme to be assisted, some risk must nevertheless be taken by the State. Loans granted only on unimpeachable security will not be sufficient for the purpose.

It is the very essence of the garden city from the economic point of view that development should be reasonably rapid ; only in this way can the amount of interest placed to capital be prevented from accumulating too rapidly in the early days. Forces, therefore, must be set in motion which will direct industry and population to the new garden cities as opposed to sporadic and haphazard development on the outskirts of the large towns and ribbons along the main roads radiating from them. So far the evidence given to Lord Marley's Committee.

Statutory recognition makes a difference in England, though nine people out of ten might find it difficult to give good reason for it. Certainly Ebenezer Howard, founder of a movement which had received Statutary recognition, was somehow a more important man than he had been as founder of Letchworth. He was talked about as one of the makers of twentieth-century England. People associated his name with a public movement even when they could not remember what the movement was or why it existed or what it was to do. By the time Welwyn was on its feet people who knew what was going on behind the scenes were looking in the birthday list of Honours for Ebenezer Howard's name.

Monsieur Benoit-Levy, whose book is mentioned elsewhere, describes Mr. Howard's work at Welwyn with French precision and clarity. Possibly the best testimony to the International interest in the movement is to quote Benoit-Levy's own words :

### HISTORIQUE DE WELWYN

" Son histoire est bien simple ; un beau jour de 1919, M. Ebenezer Howard, se rendant en chemin de fer de Letchworth à Londres, vit une affiche annonçant la vente des fermes d'Handside et de Digswell qu'il avait souvent admirées en passant.

" Pensant que les temps étaient révolus pour la création d'une deuxième cité-jardin, M. Ebenezer Howard, sans prendre conseil de personne, emprunta rapidement 720,000 francs à quelques amis personnels, parmi lesquels le capitaine Reiss, le colonel Freemantle, député, et M. Farquharson. Cela lui permit de soutenir les enchères et de se faire adjuger le domaine.

" Mais cette somme n'était pas suffisante pour covrir le versement qu'il y avait à faire immédiatement et ce fut le représentant de M. Howard à la vente qui avança lui-même le complément nécessaire.

" M. Howard s'entendit ensuite avec Lord Salisbury, propriétaire d'Hatfield, pour qu'il lui vendit de quoi arrondir le terrain des deux fermes, et forma, ensuite, une société, avec Sir Theodore Chambers comme président, pour lancer la deuxième cité-jardin.

" Cet homme de 80 ans qui, non satisfait de sa première victoire, entreprit, au lendemain de la guerre, la creation d'une deuxième cité-jardin avec une foi et une ardeur juvénile, fut ennobli en 1927 et mourut en mai 1928 au numéro 5 de Guessens Road, ayant quitté son habitation de Letchworth pour devenir un des premiers résidents de Welwyn."

" Le plan de Welwyn. Je n'ai pu faire qu'une esquisse bien sommaire de ce plan ; il suffira de se reporter à la reproduction

WELWYN—TREE-LINED ROAD, SHOWING FORMAL ARRANGEMENT OF DETACHED HOUSES
WITH GARDENS

que j'en donne pour se rendre compte que M. Louis de Soissons, l'architecte, a traité son sujet en artiste et en maître.

" Très intelligiblement, on a dessiné les lignes principales de toute la cité-jardin mais on s'est imposé de n'opérer le lotissement qu'au fur et à mesure de son developpement en procédant par l'aménagement de quartiers entiers.

" Il etait naturel de commencer par ceux situés près de la gare et non loin des usines.

" Les contours ont été soigneusement relevés et il en a été tenu compte pour le tracé des rues.

" Il a été fait un inventaire des arbres et chaque fois qu'il a été possible, on les a conservés précieusement.

" Le problème a résoudre était plus difficile ici qu'à Letchworth car, sans nuire à l'ordonnance générale du paysage, il s'agissait de loger plus de gens sur un espace moindre.

" La nouvelle ville, telle qu'elle nous apparaît actuellement forme déjà un ensemble harmonieux.

" Les centres des différentes activités ont été placé à des points stratégiques et logiques. Les différentes voies publiques s'adaptent aux usages auxquels elles sont destinées et varient en largeur et en coupe suivant les circonstances, depuis l'avenue du parc qui a cent mètres de large jusqu'aux chemins d'accès aux groupements intérieurs d'habitations qui n'ont pas plus de deux mètres de large."

## § WYTHENSHAWE—CONTRIBUTION BY LADY (E. D.) SIMON

If we desire a strong and healthy race we must encourage as large a proportion of our people as possible to live on the land.

*Report of Verney Committee, 1916.*

For those interested in the movement as a whole it is important to include its latest development—a Garden Town promoted by the Corporation of Manchester. This supplements the experience of Welwyn. The importance of Wythenshawe is that it illustrates a fresh *modus operandi* in starting Garden Cities, surmounts an obstacle which seemed to block the way. A City Corporation, having elastic credit for work which will ultimately be remunerative to the City, can cover the first years which are all expenditure by a simple credit operation, and the more freely and wisely it spends the sooner will the ratepayers find the multiple and substantial rewards of their enterprise in having created for the city new forms of wealth and new standards of well-being. Incidentally the establishment of Wythenshawe after the death of Sir Ebenezer Howard is valuable evidence of the vitality of the movement. It is evidence of progress under its own motive power, though the inspiration and energy of its founder has been withdrawn. If it can reproduce what Benoit-Levy calls the " soul " of Letchworth, which the people of that town know as the " spirit of the place," its contribution will be second to none. No one is better qualified than Lady Simon to write about Wythenshawe. The purchase and presentation to the City of Manchester of Wythenshawe Hall and its surrounding park of 250 acres by Sir Ernest and Lady Simon was an initial step in getting the project for a Garden Town started and accepted in Manchester. She has been a member of the Committee responsible for supervision and development of the Estate and chairman since 1931. Her ready response to a request to contribute an account of the progress is only an additional instance of her public spirited interest in the movement. She writes as follows :—

The latest phase of the Garden City movement is to be found in the development of a satellite garden town by the City of Manchester.

Wythenshawe differs from Letchworth and Welwyn in two important aspects. The land was acquired because there was not enough land within the City boundaries available for houses that were urgently needed for the post-war housing campaign and, instead of forming a company and raising the money from the public, the necessary capital was provided by the Corporation. Thus the bridging of the gap between expenditure and the return in the form of ground rents, which is inevitable in the early years, is made easier.

The Tatton Estate of 2,568 acres, which lay in the three parishes of Northenden, Northern Etchells and Baguley, which comprise 5,567 acres altogether, was purchased in 1926, and since that date other land amounting to 1041 acres has been added to it. Including the sites of hospitals, schools, housing estates, etc., the Corporation now owns 3,621 acres within the three parishes, or 65 per cent. of the area.

A Town Plan of the three parishes was prepared, and in 1930 Parliamentary powers were obtained by which this area was added to the City as the Wythenshawe Ward.

When the Estate was purchased by the Corporation a special

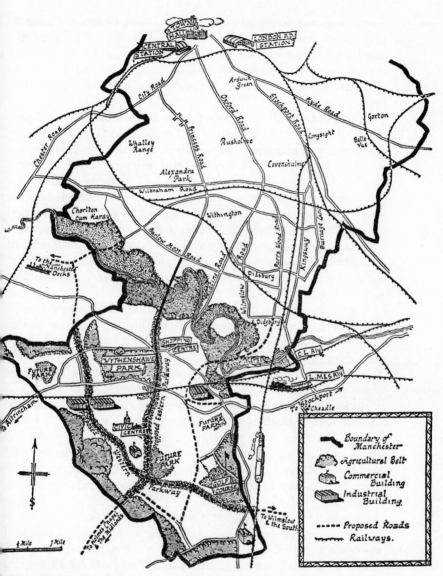

WYTHENSHAWE IN RELATION TO OTHER PARTS OF THE CITY OF MANCHESTER

Committee was formed to manage it. This Committee consists of fourteen members, and acts in the capacity of a landowner developing his estate. It arranges with the other Corporation Committees for providing the necessary services, and leases land for houses, schools, libraries, fire-stations, etc., to the appropriate Committee.

Unlike Letchworth and Welwyn, the Corporation does not own the whole area. An application was made in 1931 to the Minister of Health, under section 16 of the Town Planning Act 1925, for the acquisition of about 1,307 acres of undeveloped land lying within the Wythenshawe Ward which would ultimately be required for purposes of development. This application was refused, and the value of these pieces of land, closely adjacent to land being developed by the City, has increased in value and will continue to increase. Ownership is desirable not only to secure for the City the increment in land values due to expenditure from the rates, but also to control development in a way that is not possible under Town Planning powers alone.

Wythenshawe is not only in the line of direct descent from Ebenezer Howard's original conception, but is still more closely bound up with Letchworth. The first step taken by the Corporation after it had purchased the Tatton Estate was to engage Mr. Barry Parker of Letchworth to prepare the Town Plan for the three parishes.

Wythenshawe Hall and the surrounding Park of 250 acres had already been presented to the Corporation to be used as a Public Park. The Town Plan provided for residential land all round the Park, and for two Parkways, one on the east and one on the west side to cut through the estate, crossing near the southern boundary, and leading in to the City by Princess Road and by the Docks.

An agricultural belt of 1,000 acres has been planned, as far as existing development permits, and in the south-eastern portion of the estate there will be a municipal golf course adjoining Peel Hall. A railway from Altrincham to Stockport runs through the Estate, and two industrial zones comprising 216 acres have been set aside adjoining this line. Sites for schools—junior, senior and secondary, for libraries, swimming baths, fire station, churches, cinemas and public-houses have been allocated.

On the various shopping centres throughout the estate, the

PRIVATE DEVELOPMENT, WYTHENSHAWE

Wythenshawe Committee has built fifty-two shops which are let on leases of 5 to 21 years.

Although Wythenshawe was acquired primarily to provide for the houses that would have to be built if Manchester's housing problem were ever to be solved, it was never intended that it should be only a municipal housing estate. The garden city ideal of mixing all kinds of people in a carefully planned and co-ordinated unit has been the City's ideal, and land has been zoned for houses eight, six and four as well as twelve and ten to the acre, When completed the estate will consist of 25,000 houses of which 20,000 will be twelve and ten to the acre. Private building of houses for sale has already begun, and there are signs that it will develop rapidly.

Wythenshawe has copied its predecessors in refusing to sell land outright. Residential leases are granted for 999 years, but others for 99. The elevations of any buildings erected on land belonging to the Committee have to be submitted to Mr. Barry Parker, whose services, now that the Town Plan is completed, are retained in a consultative capacity to the great benefit of the appearance of the estate.

If Wythenshawe is at a disadvantage as compared with Letchworth and Welwyn, in that the Corporation does not own all the land, it has many advantages. There is no difficulty about raising the necessary capital for development, and all the services, main drainage, public health, education, police, swimming baths, libraries, etc., as well as the supply of water, gas and electricity, can be provided at low cost when they are an extension of existing services, and so we have not to carry the whole capital burden, which would be the case if they had to be specially provided for the area. In the same way the administrative charges for the development and management of the estate are much lower than in the case of either Letchworth or Welwyn. There has been no increase in the number of chief officials in Manchester to deal with the added area, and only a small addition to their staffs.

The following figures may be of interest. The cost to the rates of the development of the estate which was £8,629 in 1927–8, being the difference between the interest and sinking fund on the purchase and the rents received from the farms, rose to £18,382 in 1931–2 as more land was acquired and residential roads and sewers were provided.

If development proceeds as at present, it will not be long before this account shows a profit. In the figures given no account has, of course, been taken of the services which the City as the Local Authority has to provide, and which are always paid for out of the rates.

Until the Wythenshawe area was added to the City, in 1931, development had to be slow, but it is possible now to state what the position will be by the end of the financial year 1933. 4,600 houses will have been erected by the Corporation and 270 by private enterprise. These, with the houses already in existence in 1931, will mean that the estate will have a population of 20,000, out of an estimated total of 100,000. The further development depends upon many factors, such as: how far private builders, and those people who build their own houses and wish to live near Manchester—the centre of the estate is about 6 miles from the Town Hall—will be attracted to Wythenshawe; the policy of the City with regard to re-housing the people turned out by slum clearance schemes; the policy of the Government with regard to working-class houses; whether or not they restore the Wheatley subsidy, which would enable the City to build new houses more quickly than is possible if it can only work under the Greenwood Act; the recovery of industry so that new factories will be built. It is impossible therefore to forecast the future with any accuracy, but it is clear that Wythenshawe will develop differently from Letchworth and Welwyn. The population aimed at is larger, i.e. 100,000 as against 30,000 or 50,000. In a few months' time there will be more people on the estate than on either of its two predecessors.

It will be a satellite garden town, not a garden city, and as such will be closely knit with Manchester by more than financial ties. Even when factories on the spot give employment to those living around, many of the residents will continue to go to Manchester every day, and although junior, senior and secondary schools will be provided on the estate, those who want to go to the University, the College of Technology, School of Art, or similar institutions will all go into Manchester. The chief hospitals also will be in Manchester. But a population of 100,000 in an area further from Manchester than any of its existing suburbs, separated from the parent City by the River Mersey, and planned to be largely self-contained, will probably develop a life of its own. For many of its earliest and most formative years, the majority of the population of the estate will be men,

women and children who will have come straight out from the
overcrowded and sordid districts of Manchester to a well-planned
estate with gardens, and open country within easy reach. They
will build up a new life under new conditions and, in this way
Wythenshawe is perhaps carrying out Ebenezer Howard's ideal
more closely than even Letchworth and Welwyn, where the population of working-class houses is only two-fifths of the whole. He
lived to see the beginning of another form of his conception—the
promotion of a satellite town by a municipality, which means that
development can be much more rapid than in the case of the other
garden cities.

## § EARSWICK

The stability and physical strength of a nation depend largely on those
classes who have either been born or brought up in the country or have had
the advantage of country life.

*Verney Committee, 1916.*

Sir Lawrence Weaver describes the special features of Earswick :

' Earswick is a peculiarly interesting example of the benefits
of sound design, because it is both pre-war and post-war. Development has been and will be continuous and steady, and it has been
in the same hands from the start. In 1904 the Joseph Rowntree
Village Trust was created by Mr. Rowntree, and the capital with
which the enterprise has been carried on was his free gift. All
income derived from the village must be devoted to its improvement and extension. Each year, therefore, the income increases
snowball fashion and the speed of growth increases. *Given a
thousand years, and Earswick will spread all over Yorkshire.* Also,
it is not reserved for employees of the Rowntree works, who only
represent about half the Earswick population. The trustees'
motto is " First come, first served." The original lay-out was by
Dr. Raymond Unwin and Mr. Barry Parker, and when Dr. Unwin
placed his experience at the disposal of the Government, Mr. Parker
carried on. So Earswick has been the field of countless experiments and developments in detail.

' The plan of the village is on open lines, but that does not mean
extravagant lines. If speculative builders knew their business,
Earswick would be a Mecca for the shrewdest of them, because it
shows that the old way of laying out houses in dreary terraces in
parallel streets is not only ugly and unhygienic but uneconomical.

L

Mr. Barry Parker claims that the crowding of more houses on an acre than the amenities demand is only an ignorant way of wasting money : and that is true of an ordinary village or suburb where land is a reasonable price.   It would obviously not be true of costly land in a city.   But in most housing schemes the cost of the land is not the important factor, but the money spent on roads, sewers and other services.   The old speculative builder was devoted to " back additions," but they shut out sunlight, where as a projection of the plan to the front absorbs no more frontage and eliminates waste passage-space.   Intelligent planning of sites and roads, moreover, actually saves cross-roads without reducing the number of houses per acre, and yields vistas and street pictures instead of a dreary uniformity.'

# XVI

## THE STATUTORY POSITION IN 1933

*The right to government is prior to the right to self-government.*
*Elihu Root.*

ACCORDING to established precedent the factors in a new civilisation are partly Law and partly Gospel. Mr. Howard was by nature a " hot gospeller " (the St. Paul of the movement), but he had a proper respect for law and welcomed all steps which put Garden Cities within the protection and safeguards of the Statute Book.

## 1920

This year saw the first semi-official appearance of the name Garden City, paradoxically enough in an interim report to the Minister of Health, by the *Unhealthy* Areas Committee.

" We suggest that there should be encouraged the starting of new industries, and the removal of existing factories, to garden cities which should be founded in the country where the inhabitants can live close to their work under the best possible conditions."

## 1925

A Royal Commission on Local Government received evidence from the Garden Cities and Town Planning Association. It was pointed out that several large Corporations were developing residential estates outside their boundaries which lacked the essential features of the garden city owing to difficulties arising under existing laws. If these difficulties could be overcome areas could be developed as garden cities.

## 1919

Housing (Additional Powers) Act. A section provided for the acquisition of land by compulsion if necessary for housing schemes.

## 1921

Housing Act.  Section 7 enabled the Public Works Loan Board to lend money on first mortgage to authorised Associations for the purpose of developing garden city schemes.

## 1925

Town-Planning Act.  Clause 16 consolidated the two Acts mentioned.

## 1932

Town and Country Planning Act.  Clause 35 passed through Standing Committee A of the House of Commons and through the House without any amendment.  It reads :

" Where the Minister is satisfied that any local authority, or two or more local authorities jointly, or any authorised association, are prepared to purchase any land and develop it as a garden city . . . and have funds available for this purpose he may with the consent of the Treasury and after consultation with the Board of Trade, the Minister of Agriculture and Fisheries, and the Minister of Transport, acquire that land on behalf of the authority or association, either by agreement or compulsorily, in any case in which it appears to the Minister necessary or expedient so to do for the purpose of securing the development of the land as aforesaid and may do all such things as may be necessary to vest the land so acquired in the local authority or association."

In this section ' local authority ' includes a County Council.  The expression ' Garden City ' includes garden suburb or garden village, and ' authorised association ' means any society, company, or body of persons approved by the Minister whose objects include the promotion, formation, or management of garden cities, and the erection, improvement, or management of buildings for the working classes and others, and which does not trade for profit, or whose constitution forbids the issue of any share or loan capital with interest or dividend exceeding the rate for the time being fixed by the Treasury.

Mr. Loftus Hare, Editor of *Town and Country Planning*, summarises the legal position of Letchworth and Welwyn in the following paragraphs :

'Before dismissing altogether the legal aspect of garden cities, I must refer to the very interesting fact that the town plans of Letchworth and Welwyn Garden Cities, made in 1904 and 1920, respectively, were non-statutory. The first was made before the Act of 1909, and the second after the Act of 1919. The Acts could not apply compulsorily to the rural districts in which the two garden cities were to be sited ; the land was most *unlikely* to be used for building purposes—until the eyes of the two companies were focussed upon it. When, therefore, the two plans were made, they were of the nature of private estate development.

'Nevertheless, regarded as "town-planning schemes"—which they really were in every sense—they could have come under the Acts if the local authorities concerned and the owners together had seen fit to have it so. Section 54 (2) of the 1909 Act gave power to the Local Government Board "to authorise a local authority to adopt . . . any such scheme proposed by all or any of the owners of any land with respect to which the local authority might themselves have been authorised to prepare a scheme." Here were owners of 3,800 acres in Hitchin R.D.C., for which they had made a "scheme" more ambitious than any in living memory hitherto. The local authority did not move, the Local Government Board remained immobile, and the owners went forward.

'The power to adopt an owner's scheme was continued in Section 42 (2) (*b*) of the Act of 1919, but was not applied to Letchworth, nor to Welwyn. Section 2 (1) (*b*) of the 1925 Act repeats the power ; but the companies are still independent of the Acts. The words appear again in Section 6 (1) (*b*) of the 1932 Act, which represents the highwater mark of legislative achievement so far.

## 1932

'The legal position of the two Garden City Companies under the 1932 Act appears to be as follows : The built and the unbuilt portions of the two estates were already planned ; the outlying area of the Urban District Council had not been planned. The Urban District Council could pass a resolution deciding to *adopt* the scheme of the planned portion, and to *prepare* a scheme for the unplanned portion ; while the Minister would not approve this resolution until a public inquiry has been held, at which the views of the companies would be heard.'

'Meanwhile, it is understood, the Letchworth Urban District

Council has agreed not to make use of the powers under the Act so long as the First Garden City Company continues to manage the Estate and to act as the planning authority.'

Legal definition could hardly show more clearly than this the influence of Mr. Howard's great experiment. The obvious intention is to open a constitutional door for the entrance of other Ebenezer Howards. It is for the new Britain now coming to maturity to supply the new Ebenezer Howards.

> We must have many Howard-minded men
> A city is not builded in a day
> And they must do their work and come and go
> While countless generations pass away.

**LETCHWORTH**

*Photograph from the Air, showing Layout of Workers' Houses and Factories*

157

# XVII

## AN INTERNATIONAL MOVEMENT

Good ideas are contagious if they come when they are wanted. The Garden City Association having given birth to Letchworth soon realised that it had other work to do. Enquiries from all parts of England, Scotland, and Wales came pouring in which indicated that other towns and associations wanted to share in the good idea. The Garden City Association became the Garden Cities and Town Planning Association with a national function as an advisory and propagandist body. When faith or money failed to rise to the full Garden City ideal, Garden Suburbs began to spring up—dormitories and nurseries on the outskirts of growing towns. Where a suburb was out of reach, Garden Villages became popular. Sir Ebenezer Howard was idealist enough to recognise that each of these had a place and a different place in the movement he had set on foot. One star differeth from another star in glory. He drew up a clear definition of the difference between the three types of planned community in terms which deserve more general recognition than they have received.

' A Garden City is a self-contained town, industrial, agricultural, residential, planned as a whole, and occupying land sufficient to provide garden-surrounded homes for at least thirty thousand persons, as well as a wide belt of open fields. It combines advantages of both town and country, and prepares the way for a national movement, stemming the tide of population now leaving the country-side and sweeping into overcrowded cities.

' A Garden Suburb provides that the normal growth of existing cities shall be on healthy lines : such suburbs are most useful, though on the other hand they tend to drive the country yet further afield, and do not deal with the root evil, rural depopulation.

' Garden villages such as Bournville and Port Sunlight are Garden Cities in miniature, but depend on some neighbouring city for water, light and drainage : they have not the valuable provision of a protective belt, and are usually the centre of one great industry only.'

Suburbs, villages and cities became sadly mixed up in the popular mind, with results detrimental to the movement, and things became worse when speculative builders and companies began to use these names as attractions to estates which had no substantial claim to them.    If imitation is the homage which vice pays to virtue it was a tribute to the Garden City movement that it had raised the standard of taste in building and house room all over the country ; but also imitations dilute the standard of the genuine article.    Few people realise that there are only two towns which in this respect can be said to start at " scratch."

How earnestly Mr. Howard contended for the preservation of the Garden City ideal from confusion with any of the substitutes which were recommended as " just as good " appears in the following letter :

*21st June*, 1919.

The Editor,
    The *Daily Telegraph.*
Sir,

### *L.C.C. Housing Schemes.*

Will you allow me to protest against the use of the term " Garden City " as applied to the Tottenham Housing Scheme in your issue of to-day ?    It is a complete misnomer.    True, the Act of 1912 speaks of the land as to be laid out on the lines of a Garden City. But that was because neither the framers of the Bill, nor the Committee who passed it, knew what the term " Garden City " implied.

I was the first to use the term in my book *To-morrow*, published in 1898, and I applied it to new towns to be carefully planned right away in the open country with a view to attracting industries from the over-crowded cities, and of providing homes for the people near to the scene of their daily work—each town to be surrounded by a permanent belt of agricultural land, so that its inhabitants should enjoy for all time the combined advantages of town and country life.    But the phrase " Garden City " quickly caught on, and soon became used for all sorts of housing ventures and building speculations, some of little, some of very substantial value.    But this loose use of the term " Garden City " has tended most seriously to prevent our Press and our people from realising that the first and at present the only Garden City at Letchworth, Herts, is an invention of supreme importance, preparing the way, as it most certainly will, for a real and splendid solution of the housing problem, the traffic problem, the health problem, the labour problem.

A second venture on these lines will very shortly be set on foot, and profiting by the inevitable mistakes and short-comings of a first attempt, we shall then give the whole world a lesson in the art of city building which it cannot fail to understand, and to yet further develop and improve upon. As Stephenson's " Rocket " running on a short line of rails, was followed by modern locomotives crossing mighty continents, so will Letchworth prove to be the forerunner of a vast and beneficent evolutionary process, making for lasting peace and true prosperity throughout the whole world.

Yours faithfully,

(*Sgd.*) EBENEZER HOWARD.

### § TOWN PLANNING

If you have two loaves sell one and buy a lily.
*Chinese Proverb.*

The feature common to Garden Cities, suburbs and villages was that they were all pre-planned. In the words of Mr. Howard : " The essential thing is that before a sod is cut, or a brick laid, the town must in its broad outlines be properly planned with an eye to the convenience of the community as a whole, the preservation of natural beauties, the utmost degree of healthfulness and proper regard to communication with the surrounding district." Town planning was obviously a principle which had a much wider application than Garden Cities and it rapidly became the outstanding and most far-reaching feature of the movement.

To avoid the charge of exaggeration it should be said emphatically, though for many people it need not be said at all, that town planning is almost as old as towns themselves. The Greeks had definite ideas about the size and desirable forms a city should take. The Romans were always town planners. Rome has been planned and replanned through the centuries. In Venice, Verona, Milan, marvels of town planning ingenuity can be traced. In England Verulam, Silchester, Colchester, Chester and London are now laboriously recovering plans which show both conventional order and individual ingenuity. Karlsruhe, Edinburgh, Philadelphia, to take examples from various parts of the world, are cases where

town planners have been justified by their works.  The idea that
the plan of a city shows the civic intelligence and character of the
citizens is a historians' platitude.  The survivals of ancient civilisation in Peru show quite elaborate town planning in the cities of
a lost civilisation.  In more recent times Sir Christopher Wren in
England and Baron Hausmann in Paris had tried to revive the
ancient art, but unfortunately for England Wren's genius died
with him and he left no successor.  Vienna and other European
capitals were replanned in the middle of last century.  Parts of
Berlin have been " Hausmannised."  Indeed it might be said with
truth that the idea of leaving towns to grow higgledy-piggledy, or
" go as you please," is a recent lapse from civic decorum which
could only have arisen in a time when people were too busy making
money to think of anything else.  Old English villages built round
a village green are on a different plane of civilisation and æsthetic
culture from the long straggling rows of rabbit-hutch and matchbox
houses which serve the inhabitants of industrial towns to sleep and
eat in during the brief intervals between work and cinema shows.
The same contrast may be seen in America, where the old villages of
New England in Connecticut, Massachusetts and Vermont have
perpetuated the beautiful features of Old England, and are a start-
ling rebuke to the industrial horrors too numerous to mention which
show how people can forget themselves when they discern fortunes
in sight.

What happened in Howard's movement was that the Town-
planned Garden City of Letchworth, the talk and literature about
it, stirred ancestral memories of order and decency throughout
Europe.  It attracted people who had been silently in rebellion
against nineteenth-century industrialism, as they saw it obliterating
the very foundations on which their civic history, association, and
pride had rested.  Belgium, France, Germany soon had associations in fellowship with the Garden Cities and Town Planning
Association.  The movement became International and was
presently on the way to become world wide.

A particularly happy effect of the movement was seen in the
British Dominions and Colonies where towns are in the making
that have a long future before them.  In Canada, Australia and
New Zealand town planning arrived in time to make a difference
to the history of those younger Britains.  Mr. Thomas Adams,
the first official Secretary of the Letchworth Garden City, became

COTTAGES OF A MANSARD TYPE, WYTHENSHAWE

162

Town Planning Adviser to the Canadian Government, and later the Director of the Greater New York Regional Survey. In Australia, Canberra, seat of the Australian Government, was laid out by town planners on a modern design town-planned from the first sod, and one of its avenues was named after Ebenezer Howard. The New Zealand Government appointed a town planner who had been through an architect's office in Letchworth. The Malay Government appointed another with similar qualifications. Mr. John Nolen of Boston, who afterwards succeeded Mr. Howard as President of the Town Planning Association, took over the Letchworth idea and adapted it in many forms to the needs of the United States. In a few cases a definite effort was made to adopt the full programme of Letchworth Garden City. At Radburn, which lies between Patterson and Hackensack in New Jersey, the City Housing Corporation of New York has built a town on Mr. Howard's principles which has special relevance to the problems created in America by automobiles. The chairman, Mr. Bing, had corresponded with Mr. Howard, was a member of the International Federation of Town Planning Associations, visited Letchworth, took full plans and details of the Letchworth plan to New York, in order to establish a genuine Garden City. The Corporation bought a thousand acres of land at a price about ten times the price paid for Letchworth land. The dividend is limited to 6 per cent. Twenty-five thousand inhabitants were to be provided for. There are neighbourhood shopping centres. The residential part of the town is grouped round a system of parkways and garden paths for pedestrians. The houses are arranged in groups to accommodate 600 families, each group provided with a school, and occupying a block about half a mile square. Residents are able to do most of their shopping without crossing any street open to motor traffic. Through traffic is carried by broad country roads running through the estate. To maintain contact between all parts of the town underpasses are provided so that anyone may cross a main road without fear or danger. To avoid noise and smells the blocks of houses are placed on short " dead " streets—culs-de-sac—debouching on the main auto roads for through traffic. Children may go to school or to their public playgrounds, baths, etc., without needing to cross a main highway. " It is time to plan," says Mr. Stuart Chase in the New York *Times*, " consciously and deliberately communities for the motor age. The time has come to lay out

towns where children will not be run over going to school : where
suburbia may walk to the station without being frightened out of
its wits ; where one does not have to take twenty minutes to drive
a mile on a main street, where one can park a car somewhere less
than a mile from your objective, where carbon monoxide gets
plenty of chance to dissipate in plenty of air ; where street traffic
noise is at a minimum, and where houses are built with garages as
prominently in mind as bath-rooms."

Radburn lies so close to its two rapidly growing industrial neighbours, Patterson and Hackensack, and has been brought so near
to New York by the new suspension bridge over the Hudson, that
it is more likely to develop as a dormitory town than an industrial
centre, but its definite purpose as a " town for the motor age "
makes it a valuable contribution to the housing problems of the
twentieth century. A complete change in the transport habits of
the world, minimising distance, changing the meaning of neighbourhood, modifying the established habits of generations, is bound to
be reflected in the housing and civic organisation of the generation
now growing up. Radburn indicates one of the directions in which
that modification is most likely to take place. It is certain that
the changes involved will not be adequately handled by a multitude
of regulations and traffic signals. To the science and art of agriculture and horticulture must now be added " urbiculture."

It is a curiosity of nomenclature that Radburn bears the name
of a Hertfordshire town with a slight variation of spelling. With
Letchworth, Welwyn and Radburn standing for stages in the
development of the new science it looks as if Hertfordshire would
be historically identified with this step in civilisation.

The following letter from Sir Ebenezer Howard, written after
he had been Knighted, to Mr. Bing, indicates his interest in the
experiment :

23 *March* 1927.

Mr. A. M. Bing,
City Housing Corporation,
587, Fifth Avenue,
New York.

DEAR MR. BING,

Very many thanks for your kind letter in which Mrs. Bing so
kindly joined with you.

I am, as you know, immensely interested in your problem of

launching a Garden City in the United States, and have long seen
very clearly that the work you are engaged in is very valuable as a
preparation for that great undertaking, and I cannot but feel that
the time for this should not be far off.

As I recall the lunch in the City Hall of New York, and the
dinner at the Somerset Club of Boston, nearly two years ago, I
often feel I should like to come to America to aid in accomplishing
this result.   But there is much for me to do here.   It is, however,
rather likely I shall visit the States again in the Fall of this year
or the early Spring of 1928.

Yours very truly,<br>
Ebenezer Howard.

Mr. Montagu Harris, of the Ministry of Health, who has been
associated with the movement from early days, contributes the
following notes on International development :

' Howard's book was translated into many languages.   Before
the International Garden Cities Association came into existence in
1913, propaganda societies, including the words " Garden City " or
its equivalent in their titles, had been established in Austria, Australia, Belgium, France, Germany, Holland, Poland, Russia, Spain
and the United States.

' As President of the International Garden Cities and Town
Planning Association, no other person than Mr. Howard was conceivable in the eyes of foreigners, during his lifetime.   The re-
ception accorded to him at any meeting of foreigners which he
attended was always most enthusiastic.   His attitude of mind was
always sympathetic to such an audience, his ideas were recognised
as universally applicable.   A quotation from his first presidential
address to the International Association will illustrate this.

' " He was certain," he said, " that many years could not pass
by before in France, Germany, Austria, Spain, Italy, the United
States and other countries, as well as in Greater Britain, there
would arise really national Garden Cities, designed to express the
new and higher sentiments, the nobler thoughts and ambitions,
the greater control over the forces of Nature, which would more
and more characterise this our twentieth century.   The more
widely and deeply and intelligently our plans were laid, the warmer
the glow of our public spirit, the deeper our love for humanity, the

more complete our faith in the Divine ordering of this world, the sooner and more completely should we overcome all these disturbing elements which jar upon the peace of the world.  He was over-joyed to know that there had been already found so large an army of peaceful pioneers as was gathered there before him, joined to-gether from among many nations of the earth to do battle for the great cause of Man—whose cause is also the cause of the Woman and the Child, and of Nations yet unborn."

' It may be said '—adds Mr. Harris—' that the assumptions here made have not been justified by the event.  It is true enough that no Letchworth or Welwyn has yet come into existence in any other country.  The term " Garden City " has been applied, even more often abroad than at home, to enterprises which are not in accord with the full principle.  The " cités-jardins," established by the Department of the Seine, are no more than garden suburbs. There is even now no " Gartenstadt " in Germany which actually bears or is entitled to that name.  The " Ciudad Lineal " of Madrid, while it realises several garden city principles, distinctly breaks away from others.  Radburn, in the neighbourhood of New York, is a Hampstead rather than a Letchworth.'

Meanwhile, notwithstanding all qualifications, the International Garden Cities and Town Planning Association steadily increases in importance, and world-wide recognition.  Town Planning becomes more of a science and more of an art.  The idea grows and takes deeper root whether the soil be India, Russia, Japan, Australia or California, Italy or Germany.

Among Sir Ebenezer Howard's papers are notes of a speech (undated but probably in 1923) delivered at the Grand Hotel, Cannes, with Lord Wemyss in the Chair.  After references to the establishment of Letchworth and Welwyn, he gives scope to his ideals for the Movement.  As an expression of his international outlook the speech has special value, covering as it does a wider range than he allowed himself in addressing British audiences.

' But the Garden City Association is by no means going to rest on its oars.  Indeed its vast work has only just begun.

' Recently a remarkably fine site has been acquired by the Welwyn Garden City Company—a site very much nearer London than Letchworth—but at a cost per acre rather less, and this is on the main line of the Great Northern Railway.  Presently Sir

A BLOCK OF FLATS, WYTHENSHAWE

M

Theodore Chambers, the Chairman of the Company which has been formed to develop that estate, will give you a description of the site and its possibilities, and will tell you of the great advantages it will offer to all classes—including, you may be sure, disabled soldiers and sailors, ex-service officers and men, and the new poor.

' I wish to refer especially to the bearing of Garden City methods on the very grave problem of Unemployment. Every one must realise that the unemployment of over 1,300,000 persons in England —and this number is steadily increasing—is putting a terrible strain on the resources of a country already exhausted by a long and terrible war. It represents too a vast amount of seething discontent in a land which was to be made fit for heroes, and is thus a serious and growing menace to the stability of Society—a menace which our self-interest if not our humanity should cause us to make every possible effort to remove. Perhaps it will help you in some measure to realise the vast extent of the problem, if you remember that the unemployed are greater in number than the population of forty towns the size of Cannes.

' Now to appeal to—shall I call it ?—the enlightened self-interest of the wealthy classes. Let me ask them to remember that this vast amount of unemployment represents a double burden on the taxpayer. He has to support these people in demoralising idleness. On the other hand, if these men and women were producing wealth, which they might be doing if properly organised, they would themselves soon be actually bearing part of the weight of taxation and reducing the National Debt—the interest upon which is so great a burden on all.

' Now our Government does not know how to solve the Unemployment problem—and doesn't claim to know. But, on the other hand, we of the Garden City movement can say this. We are at this moment showing how to make a real beginning in the solution of this vast problem—a beginning which in time will lead on to a practically complete solution if only this form of enterprise is adequately supported. For example : the building of Welwyn Garden City will employ a large amount of labour which would otherwise be idle, and it will thus lessen the amount of taxation levied for the relief of the unemployed. Then consider too how profitably that labour will be spent. It will be employed in making roads along which houses will be immediately built, in providing water supply, laying sewers, gas mains, electric light and power cables. It will thus give employment to engineers and their numerous assistants, and to a small clerical staff of men and women. And after this money has been spent in paying for labour and materials there will have been formed the basis of a new town, well conceived, properly planned, a credit to the country, an example of sound building, and above all a town which by its healthfulness will increase the energies of the people and greatly lower its infantile mortality rate. The people of this town will have to bear their share of the national burden. Further, you will have given to a large body of workers the opportunity of living under such conditions as are unattainable in London, thus tending to lessen that unrest which is so largely the result of over-crowded insanitary homes. And as those happier conditions for the workers will have been made possible by the wise action of their employers in moving their factories out of London this must tend in some degree to increase the feeling of mutuality of interest between employer and employed.

' Do you say, " Yes, but as compared with the vast magnitude of the Unemployed problem, even the building of such a delightful town with its forty thousand or so inhabitants is but a small contribution." Granted. But might it not with equal truth have been said that a single locomotive, the Rocket of George Stephenson, could only solve the problem of cheap transport within very narrow limits. The essential point was that a single successfully running steam locomotive showed conclusively how the problem of quick transit could be dealt with on a national scale. And what was the result ? One hundred and sixty-five million pounds sterling were soon afterwards voluntarily raised in a single year for the building and equipment of Railways—giving employment to hundreds of thousands of workers.

' Now, similarly, when Welwyn has completely demonstrated the far reaching advantages of the Garden City principles, this method of town building will spread with great rapidity all over the world, and will offer a safe and profitable outlet for the investment of capital and for the exercise of ability, skill, talent and industry of every conceivable kind ; and at such a trumpet call may we not confidently expect that all classes will unite with one heart and mind to carry forward the truly splendid task of national reconstruction.

' Even now there are signs that the practical work already done to give effect to Garden City principles is deeply influencing thought and opinion in other countries.

'A book published in the United States, called *Satellite Cities*, describing a number of suburban industrial enterprises in America, actually closes with this striking tribute to the practical value of the Garden City cause:

"It is to be hoped that we shall soon see an embodiment on our own soil of that which in the English Letchworth is giving reality to a vision—the vision of a sane and simple extension of Democracy from the realms of politics into the affairs of Industry and every-day life."

'Recently I received a letter from Mr. Lawrence Veiller, the Secretary and Director of the National Housing Association, in which he says:

'There is a strong argument for the establishment of Garden Cities to be found in the serious situation, which many large cities in America now face, of actual starvation and stoppage of all the city's functions through industrial disturbances.

'A striking case in point is my own City of New York. Only this winter the city was on the verge of starvation, not because there were not sufficient food supplies, but because owing to a strike of transport workers and railway employees, it was impossible to move the perishable food-stuffs which in the course of the daily supply of the city were on their way into the city.

'The effect of this has been not only to bring the city perilously near the verge of starvation, but also greatly to enhance the cost of food at various periods to the consuming public.

"All this," adds Mr. Veiller, "is a striking argument against the city of too large size in any country, for the large city is absolutely dependent for its very existence upon transport of all kinds."

'And in another letter to me Mr. Veiller says: "I am going to make it one of the chief activities of the coming year to try and bring you to the States to embark upon a preliminary educational campaign for the establishment of Garden Cities here."

'There are also many signs that in France and Belgium, Norway and Denmark, in Switzerland and Czechoslovakia, in Australia, in South Africa, in Japan and in the Malay States, and in many other countries there is a steadily growing recognition of the value of the Garden City in the great work of reconstruction.

'But this recognition of the value of the Garden City movement came yet earlier from France and from Belgium. Distinguished representatives of those nations, Monsieur Henri Sellier, Monsieur Auguste Bruggemann, and Monsieur Augustin Rey of Paris, and Senator E. Venek of Brussels, have long been active members of the International Garden Cities and Town Planning Association, of which I have the great honour of being the President, and those gentlemen had close relations with the parent Association in London even during the War and naturally much closer relations since.

'It seems to me, then, that it is to those countries that we should turn our hopes and expectations for the next march forward. Already in France they have what are called " Cités-Jardins," but these are in the nature of small suburbs around existing large cities rather than the entirely new towns which are, as I believe, the great hope of the future. But surely this is but a passing phase, and cannot last long, especially in countries which have been devastated as have France and Belgium.

'Now I hope I have enabled you all to realise how a tract of agricultural land in Hertfordshire has been transformed into a large and beautiful town. Sir Theodore Chambers will convince you that Welwyn will be a yet greater success. Surely, then, some parts of the devastated regions of France and Belgium should be dealt with in at least as bold and comprehensive a way. And standing here, an Englishman on the soil of France, addressing my fellow country-men and country-women gathered together in this beautiful and sunny land, asking them, as I do most earnestly to help us with capital for a great enterprise which is being carried out at Welwyn in England, primarily for the benefit of the English people, I feel I should be lacking in a right sense of gratitude for the hospitality and kindness of the French people were I not ready to make the fullest acknowledgment to France for any help thus rendered to our cause. To this end I do here solemnly pledge myself, as one who has been privileged to take an active and indeed a leading part in the establishment of two entirely new towns in my native land, to follow up that work by doing all that lies in my power that can be suggested by my good friends in France and Belgium to help on the boldest and most comprehensive lines, the great work of reconstruction in those fair lands.'

Those who heard this speech thirteen years ago probably thought

WOODHILL COURT AND PEARTREE COURT

it was a far-fetched argument that Garden Cities could have any appreciable effect on the problem of the Unemployed, but in 1933 Sir Raymond Unwin is using the same argument in pressing for twenty garden cities at various points round London. The argument would be more complete if it made plain how many small holdings or family farms of about 50 acres could be established on the agricultural belt. It would cover ground that needs to be covered if the energetic type of young manhood which for half a century has been willing to do pioneering work in Canada could be persuaded to do pioneering work in establishing garden cities in England.

## § TRAINING THE EYE FOR TOWN PLANNING

If we mean by civilisation a continuous effort to make the world a better place to live in, Town Planning and civilisation may be said to rise or decay *pari passu*. When the forces, instincts and ideals of civilisation are at their highest power, Town Planning is at its best. When Town Building is careless, slovenly, insanitary, sloppy, ugly, inconvenient, anarchic, civilisation is passing through a period of eclipse. There are indications that we may be on the threshold of a renaissance of both civilisation and Town Planning. There are, it is true, other signs, but when the signposts indicate clearly the High Road and the Low Road, it is a case of " we'll tak' the high road " whoever takes the low.

Under the Town and Country Planning Act of 1932, all land, whether urban or rural, developed or undeveloped, may be included in authorised plans. Previous Town Planning Acts were concerned only with land under development. If the new situation does liberate—as may be hoped—the planning spirit, it is all the more important to train the eye by acquaintance with what has been done well in other times and countries than our own—as well as with our own best standards. An exhibition intended to serve this purpose was prepared in July 1933 by the Head Master, S. Wilkinson, M.A., with the co-operation of H. Sandford, at the new Letchworth Grammar School and opened by F. Longswith Thompson, F.S.I., A.M.I.C.E., A.M.Inst.C.E., President of the Town Planning Institute. The catalogue illustrates several of the features of the Town Planning movement as described in this book —its antiquity, decadence, revival, and world-wide extension. Since successful Town Planning must always be a compound of history and intelligent anticipation, experience and vision, the catalogue is included here to suggest how the subject may be treated in this form. It is, of course, susceptible of varied and more elaborate treatment than is given in this catalogue.

## CATALOGUE OF SCHOOL TOWN PLANNING EXHIBITION

### ANCIENT TOWN PLANNING

1. BABYLON. From the planning of the Processional Way and the grouping of the principal buildings the Greeks were inspired to plan rectangularly.
2–4. SELINUS. A Greek City founded in 648 B.C. Rebuilt in 409 B.C. to plans by Hippodamus, who had studied the Babylonian plan.
5. PRIENE. A fine example of the " chessboard " planning of the Macedonian Age (330–13 ? B.C.)
6. ATHENS. Ancient Greek cities usually clustered round an ACROPOLIS.
7. POMPEII. Built by the Romans in 80 B.C. on the Greek " chessboard " plan.
8. AOSTA. A Roman town built by Augustus in 25 B.C. at the foot of Mont Blanc following the Greek precedent as did the plans of TIMGAD and CARTHAGE in North Africa.
9. OSTIA. The sea port of Rome rebuilt by Cæsar in A.D. 46.
10. ROMAN FORUM and BATHS OF TITUS. Imperial Rome began to beautify its cities by the provision of beautiful buildings set in well-planned surroundings.

### ROMAN AND SAXON PLANNING IN ENGLAND

11. SILCHESTER. A Roman seat of Government in England. For the first time towns in England are laid out " on the square," this denoting " order " and " government," in place of barbaric disorder.
12. VERULAMIUM. An ancient British town rebuilt by the Romans, and embodying all the Roman features.
13–15. LONDON, LINCOLN and YORK. Three plans showing clearly the care exercised by Roman Surveyors in setting out a town.
16–18. CHICHESTER, GLOUCESTER and CIRENCESTER. Roman towns still flourishing to-day and bearing evidence of their origin.
19. CIRENCESTER and DISTRICT. Plan showing Roman finds.

### SAXON AND MEDIÆVAL PLANNING

20. BYGRAVE, near BALDOCK. A Saxon Village plan.
21. ELSTOW, near BEDFORD. A Saxon Village showing the original stockaded " Ham " or Green, as it ultimately became.
22. MAP OF HITCHIN. Showing the " open fields " of Saxon origin.
23. MAP OF ASHWELL. Showing the " Fields " with their names. Northfield, etc.
24. EYNSHAM. Plan showing the influence of the Saxon " strip " on a town laid out in thirteenth century.
25. Sketches of Town Halls and Village Greens.

26. ABINGDON. Plan showing Market Place in front of Church mentioned. in Domesday Book.

27. ST. ALBANS. Five plans showing its development.

28. NORWICH. Plan showing a town encircling a castle.

29. RADNOR. An example of early English planning.

30. MONTREUIL. Example of a fortified town on a difficult site which accounts for the lack of ordered planning.

31. EDINBURGH. Drawing of the site. Note Hill Fort. (See further plans.)

32. SHREWSBURY. Plan showing influence of the site on the direction of the streets.

33. LUDLOW. A Norman Town Plan.

34. CANTERBURY. Plans of the City in the seventeenth, eighteenth and nineteenth century showing the influence of the walls and gates.

35. CANTERBURY. A portion of the City Wall saved from destruction and now preserved.

36. CHESTER. Four plans showing the growth of the City.

37. YORK. Plan showing the growth of the City.

38. LONDON. Picture plan of Walled London.

39. BRISTOL. Five plans showing development of City.

40. GRONINGA. A fortified town founded in 1024.

41. LOJA. A Moorish town founded in 890, plan governed by open firing zone and Citadel.

42. VIENNA. Founded in 1137. Plan governed by fortified wall.

43. BERLIN. Founded in 1244. Note the Unter den Linden linking the palace with the Tiergarten.

44. MUNICH. Founded in 1358 as a Monastic centre.

45. AMSTERDAM. Two plans showing the influence of the canals and fortifications.

46. MANHEIM. A seventeenth-century settlement for Protestant Refugees. A rectangular plan dominated by a castle.

47. STOCKHOLM. An ordered plan even in 1784.

48. CALCUTTA, PONDICHERRY, BATAVIA. Even in the East new towns were founded with rectangular plans.

49. MONTPAZIER. A fortified town or " Bastide " founded by Edward I in France.

50. CONWAY. A " Bastide " fortified by Edward I.

51. CARNARVON. A " Bastide " fortified by Edward I.

52. KINGSTON-ON-HULL. Established as a port by the far-seeing Edward I. Eight plans showing the growth of Hull into the important town it is to-day.

53. WINCHELSEA. Built by Edward I. The receding sea stopped the town's growth.

54. SHOREHAM. Founded in 1236. A plan governed by access to the sea. An important port in the thirteenth century.

55 and 56. SALISBURY (New Sarum). These plans show the growth of the town as founded by Bishop Poore in 1270, into a beautiful modern town. Note the fine planning around the Cathedral.

57. OXFORD. Plan showing the growth of the town. A picture plan of Oxford.

58. HITCHIN. Four plans of this very interesting old town and district.
59. HERTFORDSHIRE. Sexton's map of Hertfordshire in 1577.
60. HERTFORDSHIRE. Speed's map of Hertfordshire, 1611.

## RENAISSANCE TOWN PLANNING

61. ROME. The Piazza-del-Popolo, showing the importance of street vistas.
62. THE IDEAL CITY. An Architect's vision in 1532.
63. RICHELIEU. A new town laid out by Lemercier in 1633 for Cardinal Richelieu showing order in planning in the age of disorder.
64. RICHELIEU. Lemercier's design for the buildings in Richelieu.
65. KARLSRUHE. A "radial" lay-out in front of the Palace, providing magnificent vistas and also ease of defence against attack.
66. NANCY. A fine example of Renaissance planning. The plans and photographs show clearly the relation of the Hemicycle to the Place de la Carrière and Place Stanilus as laid out by Héré, 1757.
67. LONDONDERRY. Ordered planning for the new town of Derry to be built by the Citizens of London.
68. LONDON, 1666. Sir Christopher Wren's design for the rebuilding of London after the Great Fire. Note the fine setting St. Paul's Cathedral would have had if this plan had been carried out.
69. BATH. Nine plans of Bath showing its development. Note WOOD'S plan and the fine Renaissance planning of his day.
70. EDINBURGH. Plans of Edinburgh (remember the site plan No. 31) and photographs of John Craig's New Town. Note the fine planning which has given Edinburgh one of the finest streets in Europe.
71. EDINBURGH. Three Competition drawings for an area East of Craig's New Town dated 1817. These schemes were not carried out.
72. PARIS. Three plans of Paris, and photographs. Note the "Street rectification" carried out by Hausmann. The improvements cost an immense sum, but they made Paris one of the most beautiful cities of the world. See also photographs.
73. VIENNA.[1] Plans showing "ring roads" on the site of old fortifications.
74. MOSCOW. Plan showing successive ring road on sites of former fortifications.
75. PHILADELPHIA. A diagram of William Penn's plan. It is rectangular, and this type plan has become the accepted plan for all American Cities irrespective of the contours of the site. (See also American Section for modern planning.)
76. LONDON.—Elevational drawings of The Mall and Piccadilly.

## NINETEENTH AND TWENTIETH CENTURY PLANNING

77. EASTBOURNE. An example of privately developed Recreational town planning.

[1] Vienna Housing has recently attracted much attention. Photographs should be shown. The financial method adopted is to wipe out the capital cost on the analogy of a battleship which pays no dividends except in service rendered. Rents pay for upkeep only. Other householders in Vienna pay interest charges in rates. ED.

WELWYN—A NEW FACTORY

78. **BOURNEMOUTH.**  A further example of privately developed Recreational town planning preserving the pine trees and natural amenities.

79. **LONDON.**  Plan showing growth from Roman times, and Surface Utilisation Maps.

80. **SALTAIRE.**  One of the first " Industrial Villages " designed to give the factory worker a decent home near his work.  This scheme was carried out by Sir Titus Salt in 1856.

81. **BOURNVILLE.**  Mr. George Cadbury's scheme for providing decent homes for his workpeople with facilities for open air recreation in garden and playing field.  Founded in 1879.

82. **PORT SUNLIGHT.**  Another industrial town begun by the late Lord Leverhulme in 1888.

83. **LETCHWORTH.**

84. **EARSWICK,** near York.  A Model Village belonging to the Joseph Rowntree Village Trust, designed by Barry Parker, F.R.I.B.A., P.P.T.P.I.

85. To plan or not to plan.

### POST WAR PRIVATELY DEVELOPED TOWNS

86. **WELWYN GARDEN CITY.**  The second of the many Garden Cities Sir Ebenezer Howard visualised encircling London.

87. **KEMSLEY VILLAGE.**  An industrial Village in North East Kent adjacent to the extensive Paper Mills.  Designed by Messrs. Adams, Thompson and Fry.

88. **WYTHENSHAWE.**  The latest Garden City, adjoining and belonging to the City of Manchester.  This lay-out shows a unique treatment for main roads passing through the estate—Parkways.  Designed by Barry Parker.  (See also Parkway diagrams.)

### STATUTORY TOWN PLANNING

Towns grow by individual owners of land building a house, or making a road, or it may be opening up a large estate.  It is very seldom an individual owner considers whether his new development is going to make or mar the whole town ; in fact, it is almost impossible for him to do this if he wished to.  It does not matter how well a town has been planned to start with, individual action is likely to spoil a good beginning, and this has been done many times during the last few hundred years.

With a view to co-ordinating the individual efforts of private owners, the Local Authority can now prepare a TOWN PLANNING SCHEME for the whole of their district which is undeveloped, planning (in advance of requirements) the sites and directions of new roads, the area to be used for housing, business, factories, and " earmarking " land for open spaces, parks, recreation grounds and allotments, etc.  All this is done by the Authorities under powers granted to them by Parliament.  The first Town Planning Act to be passed was in 1909.  The last Act, the Town and Country Planning Act, came into force on April 1st last.

89. Congestion.

90. **BIRMINGHAM TOWN.**  The first Statutory Town Planning Scheme.

91. **RUISLIP-NORTHWOOD.**  The second Statutory Town Plan.

92. Ashwell Town Planning Scheme. Hitchin T.P. Scheme and Stevenage T.P. Scheme.
93. Derby Town Planning Scheme.
94. Exeter Town Planning Scheme.
95. Norwich Town Planning Scheme.
96. Eastbourne Town Planning Scheme.
97. Oxford Town Planning Scheme.
98. Rugby Town Planning Scheme.
99. Bexhill Town Planning Scheme.
100. Chester Town Planning Scheme.

As we have seen a Statutory Town Planning Scheme is prepared by a Local Authority who is able to take all the factors which affect the development of a town into consideration, and forecast, as far as it is humanly possible to do, the probable growth of a town. In the same way the potential capacities of a region must be considered, in order that one town plan in that region will fit in with another town's plan. In order to effect this, Regional Town Planning Committees have been formed and many Regional plans of an advisory nature have been prepared to assist the various local authorities in any region in preparing their town plans. To amplify the Regional Plan, Reports have been issued containing much data and of extreme interest.

101. Hertfordshire Regional Plan.
102. Leeds and Bradford Regional Plan.
103. Bristol and Bath Regional Plan.
104. South West Lancashire Regional Plan.
105. South East Sussex Regional Plan.
106. East Sussex Regional Plan.
107. West Surrey Regional Plan.
108. North East Kent Regional Plan.
109. East Kent Regional Plan.

## TOWN IMPROVEMENT SCHEMES

Local Authorities are often very desirous of improving the " built up " and therefore older portions of their towns, and works of considerable magnitude have been carried out from time to time to effect these improvements.

110. Leeds Improvement Scheme and Town Planning Exhibit.
111. The Hitchin Improvement Scheme, designed by Messrs. Bennett & Bidwell.
112. Ferrens Way, Hull. By H. Hamer, the City Engineer.

## MODELS

113. The Growth of a Town.
114. The Growth of London from Roman times to date.
115. The Communications of London.
116. A Relief Map of the Hitchin Rural District.
117. Surface Utilisation Maps of Middlesex.
118. Surface Utilisation Maps of Surrey.

119. The Hertfordshire Society's Exhibit showing what is being done by private individuals to spoil the country-side, and what can be done to prevent this.

## TOWN PLANNING ABROAD

120. NEW YORK and ENVIRONS. A very comprehensive exhibit of the planning of this great area. Aeroplane photograph of New York.
121. NEW DELHI. Plan and photographs of this most interesting Indian development prepared by Sir Edwin Lutyens.
122. CANBERRA. The new capital of the Australian Commonwealth.
123. CHICAGO. Having found by experience that the rectangular system of planning is not ideal, American Cities are being replanned as far as possible to provide greater facilities for traffic and inter-communication.
124. COLOMBO. The Town Plan.
125. CHATHAM VILLAGE, U.S.A. This Village takes its name from William Pitt Earl of Chatham and is near Pittsburgh. Its streets are designed for the " Motor Age," and its lay-out departs from the more usual American lay-out. The village is built on a sunny slope where spaciousness and restful garden afford a setting for the beautiful homes.
125B. RADBURN, NEW JERSEY. Between HACKENSACK and PATTERSON. A town for the " Motor Age." Garden City designs.
126. WASHINGTON, D.C. Laid out originally by Major L'Enfant in 1791, on a site selected by President Washington. The city has grown through the years beyond the boundaries of the original plan without control, producing conditions so serious that new highway plans for the whole of Columbia have had to be prepared from time to time, and the internal portions of the City replanned. The map and view show the Washington of the future.
127. Plan of Mount Vernon Memorial Highway.
128. The Bronx Parkway.
These plans show the roads of the future.
129. Examples of American City replanning.
130. Town Planning in Palestine.

## HOUSING

Much has been done since the War to provide homes for the lesser paid workers, by Local Authorities and Public Utility Societies.

131. The "NEW HOMES FOR OLD EXHIBITION " shows many examples of bad housing, overcrowding, the effects of overcrowding, and the efforts of the local authority and others to combat the evils of this state of things.

Particular attention should be given to the flats and tenements built by the London County Council and others in this country and the flats in Vienna, Berlin, etc. If people are housed in flats they must be given certain amenities such as wash-houses, playgrounds, etc.

132. An interesting Housing Scheme is that carried out for the Loughborough Corporation by Mr. Barry Parker, and also

133. Lay-out for the Colliery Village of Llay.
134. Lay-out for the Colliery Village of Rossington.
135. Slum clearance at Hull.

### LETCHWORTH

Great difficulty has been experienced in collecting material for this section, but through the kindness of the officials of the First Garden City Co., Mr. Westell, acting on behalf of the Museum, and the Editor of the *Citizen*, it will be possible to form an idea of the growth of Letchworth during the past thirty years.

1. Map of estate before development.
2. Three plans submitted to First Garden City Co., for original lay-out.
3. First published plan of proposed lay-out.
4. Series of maps showing development of estate.
5. Series of maps showing development of roads—gives a clear idea of rate of development.
6. Graphs showing growth of population and numbers of houses.
7. Map showing regional development of Letchworth.
8. Open spaces. Note how well planned they are for centres of population and for schools.
9. Map showing schools—again conveniently placed for pupils.
10. Aeroplane photograph " tied on " to corresponding area on map.
11. Views of Letchworth roads, ways and buildings.
11A. Factories. Interior and exterior views.
12. Views of York showing busy shopping area and attempts at street widening.
13. Views of Baldock.
14. A few scenes from days gone by.
15. Selection of views from the Museum collection. (A complete record of happenings in Letchworth is filed at the Museum and is open to inspection by the public.)
16. Model of village.
   (*a*) An agricultural hamlet.
   (*b*) Hamlet developed on haphazard lines.
   (*c*) Hamlet developed on planned lines.
17. Speed's Map of Hertfordshire and Atlas Map of N. E. Herts, 1786.
18. Map of Letchworth and District.
19. Model of Hertfordshire (made in the School).
20. Model of Letchworth (made in the School).
21. Model of Mount Everest (true to scale)—if compared with *Daily Telegraph* photograph lent by W. H. Smith & Sons, it will be seen how closely models represent surface features.
22. Welwyn Garden City Exhibit.
23. Wythenshawe Estate.
24. Photograph of Chairman of the First Garden City Co. Sir Ebenezer Howard dreamt of a Garden City, the Architects planned one, but successive Chairmen of the Company shaped the policy of those who made it possible for the dream to be realised.

# XVIII

## HONOURS

This high man with a great thing to do
Dies ere he knows it.

*Browning.*

IN 1924 Mr. Howard had been made an O.B.E., and in 1927 His
Majesty graciously conferred on him a Knighthood. The honour
was accepted as a recognition that the Garden City and Town
Planning Movement had become a National asset.

If there were any order or distinction for men who had given
their lives to making the world a little better than they found it,
Ebenezer Howard would have been included in such an order. It
is difficult to give adequate recognition of service of an original
kind rendered by men not in the regulation classes of public service.
Bernard Shaw wrote when Mr. Howard was Knighted: "He
deserved a knighthood for his book, a baronetcy for Letchworth,
and an earldom for Welwyn." These at their face value are feudal
distinctions and belong to a sphere of service with which Mr.
Howard had no affinities. Some types of human service bring a
natural return in money, and when that happens other forms of
recognition come with it. There is no material equivalent for the
deep social insight and long range vision which inspired Mr. Howard's
work. For the highest forms of service, which alter the range of
men's minds, elevate their ideals, and so absorb a man's whole
energies that he has no time or opportunity to make money there
is no appropriate reward, and in the hurry and pressure of life,
and the hurly-burly of more self-seeking characters, such men are
apt to be thrown out with the scrap as unable to take care of themselves. Possibly some day a new kind of Civil List or a new class
of stipendiary life peerages may be contrived which would make
room for distinguished servants of humanity and at the same time
remove them from the fear of the combined attack of old age and
straitened circumstances.

Meanwhile taking things as they are the Knighthood gave much satisfaction to Sir Ebenezer Howard's friends and fellow-workers in the movement. It marked another stage in the public recognition which was an essential element in success. Not often do congratulatory letters come in from such a wide area.

His early associates in the movement felt that the honour was a justification of their faith in him. France was represented by the Section Française de l'Association Internationale des cités-jardins et de l'Aménagement des villes. The British Esperanto Association sent " sinceran gratulon pri via meritita honorigo kui samtempe honoras nian mʊradon." Lord Cecil of Chelwood thought the honour should have come much earlier. Professor Paul Mijuef of the Technological Institute, Leningrad, wrote that the Leningrad Architects Society had elected Sir Ebenezer an Honorary member of that body, and Dr. Block had translated and published his book *Garden Cities of To-morrow*. From Bombay came a letter enclosing particulars of a new planned village Lalitadripuram established with the active sympathy of the local Maharajah. H. W. Hetzel wrote from Philadelphia, Pa., and W. Horn from Malacca, Straits Settlements, saying the honour was long overdue. The Institute of Shorthand Writers practising in the Supreme Court of Judicature appreciated an honour done to one of their number. Mr. Seebohm Rowntree wrote : " I have just returned from a trip round the world, and when I was in some remote spot in the East I was delighted to hear that at last the King had recognised the great services you have rendered to the cause of better housing and the development of our cities." Dr. Hans Kampffmeyer wrote from Vienna : " It makes me glad to realise that through this act the authorities officially acknowledge the importance of the movement you have created." Herr Otto of the Deutsche Gartenstadt-Gesellschaft expressed the satisfaction of German fellow-workers. Mr. Cyrus Kehr of Washington, D.C., adopts the same attitude : " This may also be taken as a recognition by the King of the importance of co-ordinated city or town development in lieu of the haphazard procedure." Herr Keppler, Director of Housing, Amsterdam, with a weight of housing achievement behind his name, joined the chorus of congratulation. The Town-Planning Association of Victoria wrote from Melbourne " to place on record its appreciation of the wonderful work done for the peoples and cities of the world and to congratulate him on the honour." Mr. Kincaid

N

telegraphed congratulations from Niagara Falls, U.S.A.; Mr. Gilbert Lang from Glasgow. Sir Walter Layton from the office of the *Economist*, and the Lord Mayor of London from the Mansion House, thought that " if we are to have honours at all they cannot be more fittingly used than to mark the appreciation of the Nation of such services as those which you have performed." Mr. Litchfield of New York wrote : " The thousands all over the world who know of your work will rejoice in this recognition of it, and to the many who knew you personally there will be deep additional satisfaction." Mr. Lloyd George telegraphed : " Delighted your great work for town planning and Garden Cities has been honoured by knighthood." Newspapers, British and Foreign, contributed a string of laudatory adjectives and comments which placed end on would have stretched the nine miles from Letchworth to Welwyn,[1] —this being what Americans call a " stretcher."

These are enough to indicate how the great fellowship of forward-looking men in all countries felt that in Sir Ebenezer Howard they had a distinguished comrade whose successful work reflected credit on the whole fellowship.

Mr. Neville Chamberlain, Minister of Health, spoke at the congratulatory dinner given to the new Knight in Letchworth, and the recipient made one of his charmingly modest speeches.

[1] See *Garden Cities and Town Planning*, February, 1927 ; May–June, 1928.

# XIX

## ET CETERA

He produces without possessing, he acts without regard to the fruits of acting.

*Lao-tsze.*

EVERY one knows that the most interesting parts of a public speech are the asides. The main current shows what the speaker intended to say, but the asides let you into the secrets of his mind and reveal the subconscious man. On the same principle Wordsworth points out that the best portions of a good man's life are

> the little nameless unremembered acts
> of kindness and of love.

Judged by this test Sir Ebenezer Howard's personality has plenty of interest, and in this chapter a few of the asides are gathered for those who are more interested in the personality of the man than in the movement he created.

The international bearings of his work made him acutely aware of the difficulties created by varieties of language. He felt the unities of fact and interest which link nations and races together, and deplored the obstacles which prevented mutual understanding. This led him to what seemed the shortest cut out of this maze, Esperanto. With his natural vigour of mind he became a typical Esperantist.

As president of the Letchworth Esperanto Society from 1911 until he left Letchworth, he took an active interest in its work. At one period a meeting for Esperanto conversation and translation was held weekly at his house.

He was also a member of the Universal Esperanto Association from 1911 to the end of his life, and regularly read *Esperanto*, the monthly magazine of that organisation, and other Esperanto literature.

He attended several of the annual International Esperanto

Congresses and, in 1907, when about five hundred members of the third International Congress, which met in Cambridge that year, visited Letchworth on August 13th, Mr. Howard welcomed them with a speech in Esperanto. The following is a translation of part of that speech :

" Friends of the young language !

" I most heartily greet you in the name of the friends of the young city. Esperanto and the Garden City are both bringing about new and better conditions of peace and agreement. Therefore it gives me great pleasure to tell you, through the medium of our dear, young language Esperanto, something about our dear young Garden-City. I do so, nowise doubting, that, as Esperanto is destined to become a language universally understood, so too the fundamental principles of the Garden City Movement will some day be applied throughout the world. Garden City aims at achieving, in the sphere of everyday life, what Esperanto aims at in the sphere of languages.

" Having purchased a new estate, four years ago, we are endeavouring to establish a new town for the benefit of all.

" The fundamental principles of Garden City, like the grammatical rules of Esperanto, are very few and easily grasped.

" The first principle is that the ground on which the town stands, must belong to its inhabitants. In order gradually to attain that result, the company limits its dividends to 5 per cent, and the remaining profit it spends on the improvement of the town. Moreover, it keeps in view the idea of handing over the whole thing at some future time to a Trust representing the inhabitants.[1] ' The land for the people,' this is the first rule of the Garden City grammar. The second principle is that urban life, with its social advantages, must be combined with rural life, with its beauty, sweetness and freshness. To effect this we placed our town in the central part of the purchased site and surrounded it with its own zone of cultivated ground. The advantage of such a system is very great. As the town increases, the cultivated area will find its own natural market. Fruit, vegetables and milk will not have

[1] At present the technical position is that the Estate Company is trustee for the inhabitants. The Company supplies financial and estate management. The town gets the benefit of improvements and the shareholders get 5 per cent. The Urban District Council discharges the usual functions of such Councils in local Government.

to be conveyed long distances, but will be enjoyed by the inhabitants themselves. On the other hand, the workers will always have the country near them, where they can enjoy the peace and quiet that Nature bestows. Besides this they will be able to alternate their work in the factory with field and garden work. 'Marriage of town and country,' this is our second rule.

" The third principle is to attract, as by a strong magnet, people from the crowded towns to districts of the land, where the inhabitants are too few to gain the benefits of association. Thus our work will at the same time strike a blow at two evils : overcrowding in towns and too sparse population of the country. The chief attractions, by means of which we aim at drawing people from the overcrowded towns are : first, work under healthy conditions, second, next inexpensive dwellings near their places of work, third opportunity for sport and amusements." [1] The stars indicate that there is more of the speech not quoted.

\*　　\*　　\*　　\*　　\*

In 1912 Mr. Howard visited the eighth International Esperanto Congress in Cracow and gave a lantern lecture on the subject of " Garden Cities."

If he had lived a little longer one can imagine him persuading Mr. Bernard Shaw to put the case for his movement into Basic English.

When he was close on seventy he was met by a Letchworth doctor sprinting along Broadway, which was then a straight mile cinder track.

" What's the hurry, Mr. Howard ? "

" I'm running for exercise. We must keep ourselves physically fit," was the reply.

" But at your age you ought not to be running. You may strain something."

" I'm sound, but I need exercise. I must keep fit."

Truth to tell, he had no outdoor pursuit that would keep him fit, but he felt the need of it as he grew more rotund. To the last he walked like a busy man acting on the sound principle : " never run for a train unless you have plenty of time and want exercise." His creative mind required some stimulus—more so as he got older. When his mind was working, his own ideas excited him. Those who watched him, sometimes anxiously, were afraid

[1] Contributed by Miss Bartholomew, 154, Wilbury Road, Letchworth.

lest some physical catastrophe might supervene. His whole body seemed to tremble and respond to the force of an idea he was expressing. Public speaking probably gave him the same kind of stimulus that many people get from outdoor sports.

He was a good reader and could always get an audience when it was announced that Mr. Ebenezer Howard would give a reading from Charles Dickens. He was particularly good in humorous parts, which may be taken as an indication that he had a sense of humour however suppressed by his more serious vocation. His voice, utterance, natural elocution and dramatic instinct would have served him well if he had gone on the stage. Chess was one of his recreations. He carried on a perennial tournament with Mr. Leakey of the Spirella—a fact which adds weight to Mr. Leakey's verdict that Sir Ebenezer Howard was a " really good chess player." On the occasion of the last talk between these old chums the question of a future life had been raised. He had the confidence which seems to belong to those who have given their lives to great and unselfish causes :

" These all died in faith, not having received the promises, but having seen them and greeted them from afar, and having confessed that they were strangers and pilgrims on the earth. For they that say such things make it manifest that they are seeking after a country of their own ; . . . they desire a better country—that is a heavenly—wherefore God is not ashamed to be called their God : for he hath prepared for them a city."

One of the winning qualities in Howard's personality was his freedom from possessive egoism—the grit that destroys co-operation more quickly than anything else. He once described a scene which is very easily pictured. He had been advised to call on an American millionaire who at that time had a house on Park Lane:

" Good morning, Mr. ——. What a marvellous outlook you have from these windows."

" That's nothing to me ; I don't own the outlook."

" But to have that beautiful Park to rest your eyes on in the midst of London must surely be a constant pleasure."

" It's nothing to me ; I don't own the Park."

" But I get lots of satisfaction in seeing things I don't own and don't want to own."

" Well, I don't—that's all. What did you want to see me for ? "

That killed the subject, but if the talk had gone on it would have become clear that Ebenezer Howard was the richer man of the two. He enjoyed things that everyone could share—the millionaire only things that were his own. As more things can be enjoyed than can ever be owned Howard had staked a claim in a larger scheme of life than his acquaintance.

Mr. Leakey records his impression of him :

" I had read soon after it appeared Howard's *Garden Cities of To-morrow* with the fanciful design of a Garden City arranged in concentric circles of streets, etc., and I had always been fascinated by its idealism, but I had never made the acquaintance of its author until about twenty years before his death.

" My brother Louis happened upon a journey home from New York to make the acquaintance of two American gentlemen who were coming to London for the first time, to introduce a patent of theirs, for which a factory had to be established.

" He introduced them to me and I at once thought of Letchworth as the very place where a factory might be placed in ideal conditions, because Howard was there trying to realise his dream of a Garden City.

" An appointment was arranged, and these two American gentlemen, my brother and I met Ebenezer Howard for the first time ; the result was the establishment at Letchworth of the Spirella corset factory that now employs nearly two thousand persons.

\*    \*    \*    \*    \*

" From that time Sir Ebenezer and I have been fast friends. His ideals attracted me, we frequently met, and on one occasion I shared his flat at Letchworth for several months while my wife and children were abroad. We played chess a good deal and he invariably beat me.

" Like myself he was practically a non-smoker and inclined to vegetarianism ; but he had a great belief in a future life about which we had many discussions, and among the last things that he said to me was, ' Whatever you may say, old Leakey, we shall meet again hereafter.' "

A man's faith is expressed in his life—and when that is so it does not add much to put it into words. To the last, Howard's form of faith was not a faith in any kind of form. Yet it served him well. He had the unfailing instinct for the higher alternative when two courses were open—meaning by higher the course which required courage, gave larger opportunity and ampler significance to what he was doing. He had a sustained ethical fervour which made him hate to see things done the wrong way when the right way was open and known. The essential quality of a prophet is insight—especially insight into the working of the ethical laws which are at the foundation of right living. That quality he had. He defined his social philosophy as *associated individualism* and his methods were generally based on principle with a polite bow to expediency. His optimism rested ultimately on belief in God —as a loving power who could not let evil triumph or good and right things be cast on the rubbish heap. He does not seem to have been a great or profound reader of books and he knew that he lacked cultural background. But he brought to the problems of life a clear and active mind that worked ceaselessly on the question—Why had civilisation produced such poor results for the majority of the race and how could it be set on a better track ? The answer he gave, " that it is necessary now to effect a new integration of nature and human nature, in obedience to the evolutionary urge, if our creative life—the highest powers of the human personality—are not to be worsted "—is so nearly identical with the answer brought by other eminent thinkers that one can only wonder and admire that the way of thought and the way of action should lead to the same goal.

Among the interesting asides are some typical letters :—

*His Shorthand Type Machine.*

NEVELLS ROAD,

LETCHWORTH, HERTS,

— SIMMONDS, Esq.,                    13*th April*, 1926.

DEAR SIR,

Mr. Ebenezer Howard has asked me to write you with reference to your son Jack.

Mr. Howard tells me that Jack has expressed a wish to work on his shorthand typewriter, and he is now able to put a proposition before you which he would be glad if you will consider.

As you may know, after many years of experimental work Mr. Howard now has a machine which he considers is ready to put on the market. For the past 18 months we have been making jigs, tools, etc., to enable the machines to be made on the most economical lines, and we are now practically ready to commence production.

Mr. Howard is having his text-books printed and expects to

have these in a very few weeks ; as soon as these are ready it will
be necessary to have one or two demonstrators of the machine
before sales can be effected, and for such a position Mr. Howard
has your son Jack in mind.

It is of course essential that a man in such a position should be
able to write and speak good English, also to spell correctly.

It would be necessary to become proficient in the use of Mr.
Howard's code. This, I believe, can be accomplished quite
speedily, while a thorough mechanical knowledge of the machine
would also be advisable ; this could of course be obtained by
spending a few weeks in this factory.

Mr. Howard is very confident of success with his machine, and
considers the prospects of anyone filling the position I have outlined to be exceptionally good.

Perhaps you will give the matter your careful consideration and
let Mr. Howard know your decision, or should you care to see a
machine or require any further information, I shall be glad to
call and see you.                    _____

*Secretary.*

5, GUESSENS ROAD,
WELWYN GARDEN CITY, HERTS,
*May* 11, 1926.

DEAR MR. SIMMONDS,

Very many thanks for your letter.

The suggestion you make seems to be a very good one, and I
should like to meet your friend. If we come to an understanding
he can certainly have a machine, also a proof of the text-book.

I have a wealthy friend in Philadelphia, who has a Secretary who
can't believe a machine can be made to equal shorthand as written
with pen or pencil and if she is converted it would go a long way.

Yours truly,
(*Signed*) EBENEZER HOWARD.

*Life and Death.*
5, GUESSENS ROAD,
WELWYN GARDEN CITY,
HERTS,
*May* 24, 1926.

DEAR MR. SIMMONDS,

I would rather (if it is convenient) call on you than have you

call on me.  There's no room at 6, Finsbury Pavement.  Let me
have your address.

I confess I am not grieved to hear that Mr. Langston has passed
away.  When we have done our work, it is not well to linger on.
I do *want* to live a bit longer, because I have something definite
I want to do ; but if I am taken sooner than I want to be, it will
still be for the best, not only for me, but for the work.

Mr. Langston certainly did more for the Garden City movement
than any other man in his position, and we shall all miss him.

I very seldom go to funerals, but I loved your wife's Father.

Yours very truly,

(Signed) EBENEZER HOWARD.

Helping a lad to find a job.

5, GUESSENS ROAD,

WELWYN GARDEN CITY,

HERTS,

June 3rd, 1926.

DEAR MR. SIMMONDS,

I have just been speaking to Mr. H. Craske, the Secretary of
First Garden City, about your boy.  I first asked him if there
were a vacancy at the Estate Office.  He thought there was in
the Accounts Department.  There he would start at eighteen
shillings and sixpence (I think he said) per week, but would be
rather quickly advanced if he did well.

Then I told him about Jack's skill (in the garage of your house)
in various directions and wondered whether there would be an
opening at the Power Station.   He could hardly express an opinion
on that point, but said that Mr. Gould took great interest in those
who showed themselves capable.

Then I told him he was the son of Mr. Langston's daughter, and
I am sure his relationship to so keen a worker as his father was
in the Garden City cause should stand him in good stead.

You should call on or write to Mr. Craske.

I enclose 18*s.* cheque.

With all good wishes to you and yours,

(Signed) EBENEZER HOWARD.

P.S.   I am writing this at King's Cross and find I am without
my cheque book—but I will send cheque when I get home.

# XX

## ALL THE TRUMPETS

*I have not found so great faith, no, not in Israel.*

*St. Luke vii. 9.*

THE remaining personal facts of Sir Ebenezer Howard's life are
soon told. In 1908 he married Miss E. A. Hayward of Letchworth,
who watched over his later years and survived him—the present
Lady Howard, of Howard Cottage, Letchworth. The surviving
children of his first marriage are : Cecil, of Messrs. Howard and
Smeaton, who carries on the established tradition as reporter in
the Law Courts which he inherited from his father ; Edith, Mrs.
Berry, who has contributed to these pages ; Kathleen, Mrs. Rawlin-
son, who lives at Welwyn Garden City ; and Margery, Mrs. Sidney
Lloyd. He had reached the age of seventy-eight and was still in
the harness created by his own good works. He had been occupying himself—perhaps too anxiously—with the accounts of the
Welwyn Stores when he was taken ill. Presently it was reported
that his illness was likely to be serious, and on May Day 1928 at
5, Guessens Road, Welwyn Garden City, he passed over.

"When he passed over," wrote Bunyan of Mr. Valiant-for-the-
Truth, "all the trumpets sounded for him on the other side."
For those whose faculties of intuition are not so keen as Bunyan's
it is something to remember that in Sir Ebenezer's case all the
trumpets sounded for him on this side. The big bass of *The Times*
led the way and papers of all parties joined the chorus. He was
a people's hero. Thousands knew him by sight or name, and to
them all he was the same—the genial, kindly, eager, spectacled
figure—slightly stooping and much occupied with what was going
on inside his busy brain—never the autocrat even of a breakfast
table—never too busy to speak kindly to an acquaintance, never
inclined to rest on his oars or parade his laurels, thinking of workers,
unemployed, strugglers, sick, needy folk, and planning to help them

if he could, instinctively brave and cautious, cheerful and con-
tented in the present but ambitious and forward looking for the
future, not putting this on as a pose but speaking and acting because he was himself like that.

In both Letchworth and Welwyn there were tributes, not mourn-
ful but triumphant, to his life ; and among these one stands out.
A very simple memorial stone stands in Letchworth in Howard
Park beside the children's wading pool at the centre of some curv-
ing seats where tired workers may sit and watch their children
play.  The inscription says :  " Ebenezer Howard founded this
town in 1903."  When this stone was unveiled Mr. Cecil Harms-
worth, friend both of the founder and the movement, said :

" We are here to-day to do honour to a very remarkable man.
To many of us he was a personal friend, and our loss when he
died was a double one.  He had that greatest gift of friendship—
an affectionate interest in his friends and their affairs.  He was
never so deeply absorbed in his own mission as to be indifferent
or careless in his private relations.

" But I am to speak of him to-day rather as a public character,
and I claim for him that he was one of the most eminent men of
his time.  I would say, too, one of the most successful.  It is a
disappointment to many men and women who play a large part
in public affairs that they often see little or no result of their labours.
They hope and believe that they have worked well but are unable
to point to any definite achievement.  This was not the case with
Ebenezer Howard.  The two Garden Cities at Letchworth and
Welwyn represent achievements far more important than those
that have resulted from the labours of more prominent men than
Ebenezer Howard.  And there are in addition the thousand and
one housing developments up and down this country and, it may
be said, all over the world, that owe their inspiration to the same
man.

" When it was proposed to establish definite memorials to
Ebenezer Howard at Letchworth and Welwyn it was questioned
by some whether the Garden Cities did not themselves constitute
his proper memorials.  They are, and always will be, his greatest
monuments.  But newer generations are growing up and there is
an ever-increasing stream of visitors to Letchworth and Welwyn
who cannot be as familiar as we are with Ebenezer Howard's work,
and who need to be reminded of it.  In view, however, of the fact

that the two Garden Cities are, as I have said, his outstanding monuments, his friends have not sought to raise in his honour costly and elaborate memorials. You will agree, I am sure, that such a simple Stone of Remembrance as we dedicate to-day is appropriate and adequate to our purpose.

" What was the secret of Ebenezer Howard's influence ? There was first his great conception of the ideal city. It might have remained buried in the humble little book in which it was first explained if Ebenezer Howard had only been a dreamer of dreams. But he was animated by an ardent enthusiasm and he had an unequalled gift for inspiring other people. Among his first sup- porters were eminent men in all the practical walks of life—Mr. George Cadbury, Lord Leverhulme, the Thomassons, Mr. Justice Neville, Mr. Justice Bailhache, Mr. J. H. Whitley, afterwards Speaker of the House of Commons, Sir Albert Spicer, Lord North- cliffe, and many others. What brought these men to his side in the earliest days when his Garden City was nothing more than open Hertfordshire country ? Their recognition, it is certain, that his idea was a noble one, that it was capable of being carried out, and that the man who thought of it was worthy on every ground of their encouragement. His zeal infected them and his transparent honesty of purpose gave them complete confidence.

" And surely no man ever had fewer material advantages in carrying out the ambition of his life. Until almost the end Ebenezer Howard was occupied day in and day out in the drudgery of a grinding and ill-paid profession. It was latterly a matter of deep concern to his friends that he was not free to devote the whole of his time to the promotion of Garden Cities. Ebenezer Howard himself did not complain. In his essentially modest and unselfish mind scarcely, if ever, arose the thought that the years spent by him in earning a precarious livelihood were years precious to humanity.

" I will conclude with this reflection. Most of us have thought of the wonderful things we could do for mankind if we had wealth, power, a commanding voice in the affairs of state. Possessing none of these things most of us resign ourselves to doing nothing. See how different it was with the man who is in our minds to-day ! He possessed no worldly advantages whatever, yet he triumphed in the cause to which he devoted the best energies of his mind and soul. That is why we assemble here this afternoon and why we rejoice, and future generations will rejoice, to do him honour."

# THE BUILDING OF OUR CITY

Let not our town be large, remembering
That little Athens was the Muses' home,
That Oxford rules the heart of London still,
That Florence gave the Renaissance to Rome.

Record it for the grandson of your son—
A city is not builded in a day:
Our little town cannot complete her soul
Till countless generations pass away.

Now let each child be joined as to a church
To her perpetual hopes, each man ordained:
Let every street be made a reverent aisle
Where Music grows and Beauty is unchained.

Let Science and Machinery and Trade
Be slaves of her, and make her all in all,
Building against our blatant restless time
An unseen, skilful, medieval wall.

Let every citizen be rich toward God.
Let Christ the beggar, teach divinity.
Let no man rule who holds his money dear.
Let this, our city, be our luxury.

*Vachel Lindsay.*

# APPENDIX

## PHILOSOPHIC BASIS OF THE TOWN PLANNING MOVEMENT

THIS book was already finished and in the hands of the Manchester University Press when Professor A. N. Whitehead's *Adventures of Ideas*, published this year (1933) by the Cambridge University Press, happened to come into my hands. His interpretation of the transition period through which we are passing is an important contribution to the much debated question whether we require an intensified urban development or a change to a semi-rural and entirely natural development with a fundamentally simplified religion and a qualitative change in dealing with the " good earth." Professor Whitehead's thinking contains some remarkable parallels to the general argument set forth less brilliantly and more prosaically in these pages, of which the following paragraphs are illustrations.

It is the essence of art to be artificial. But it is its perfection to return to nature, remaining art. In short, art is the education of nature. Thus in its broadest sense it is civilisation. For civilisation is nothing other than the unremitting aim at the major perfections of harmony (p. 349).

It is a false dichotomy to think of Nature and Man. Mankind is that factor in Nature which exhibits in its most intense form the plasticity of nature. Plasticity is the introduction of novel law. The doctrine of the Uniformity of Nature is to be ranked with the contrasted doctrine of magic and miracle, as an expression of partial truth, unguarded and unco-ordinated with the immensities of the Universe. Our interpretations of experience determine the limits of what we can do with the world (p. 99).

The creation of the world—said Plato—is the victory of persuasion over force. The worth of men consists in their liability to persuasion. They can persuade and can be persuaded by the disclosure of alternatives, the better and the worse. Civilisation is the maintenance of social order, by its own inherent persuasiveness as embodying the nobler alternative. The recourse to force, however unavoidable, is a disclosure of the failure of civilisation, either in the general society or in a remnant of individuals. Thus in a live civilisation there is always an element of unrest. For sensitiveness to ideas means curiosity, adventure, change. Civilised order survives on its merits, and is transformed by its power of recognising its imperfections (p. 105).

Throughout the whole span of civilisation up to the present moment, the growth of condensed aggregates of humans, which we call cities, has been an inseparable accompaniment of the growth of civilisation. . . .

. . . But there are disadvantages in cities. As yet no civilisation has been self-supporting.[1] Each civilisation is born, it culminates, and it decays. There is a widespread testimony that this ominous fact is due to inherent

---

[1] *Self-renewing* would better express the idea.

biological defects in the crowded life of cities.   Now, slowly and at first faintly, an opposite tendency is showing itself.   Better roads and better vehicles at first induced the wealthier classes to live on the outskirts of the cities.   The urgent need for defence had also vanished.   This tendency is now spreading rapidly downwards.   But a new set of conditions is just showing itself.   Up to the present time, throughout the eighteenth and nineteenth centuries, this new tendency placed the homes in the immediate suburbs, but concentrated manufacturing activity, business relations, government and pleasure, in the centres of the cities.   Apart from the care of children, and periods of sheer rest, the active lives were spent in the cities.   In some ways, the concentration of such activities was even more emphasised, and the homes were pushed outwards even at the cost of the discomfort of commuting.[1]   But if we examine the trend of technology during the past generation, the reasons for this concentration are largely disappearing.   Still more, the reasons for the choice of sites for cities are also altering.   Mechanical power can be transmitted for hundreds of miles, men can communicate almost instantaneously by telephone, the chiefs of great organisations can be transported by airplanes, the cinemas can produce plays in every village, music, speeches, and sermons can be broadcast.   Almost every reason for the growth of cities, concurrently with the growth of civilisation, has been profoundly modified (p. 120).

The effect of new technologies on the sites of cities, and on transformations of cities, is one of the fundamental problems which must enter into all sociological theories, including the forecasting of business relations. . . .

. . . We are faced with a fluid, shifting situation in the immediate future. Rigid maxims, a rule-of-thumb routine, and cast-iron particular doctrines will spell ruin.   The business of the future must be controlled by a somewhat different type of men to that of previous centuries.   The type is already changing, and has already changed so far as the leaders are concerned (p. 122).

Mankind can flourish in the lower stages of life with merely barbaric flashes of thought.   But when civilisation culminates, the absence of a co-ordinating philosophy of life, spread throughout the community, spells decadence, boredom, and the slackening of effort.

Every epoch has its character determined by the way its populations react to the material events which they encounter.   This reaction is determined by their basic beliefs—by their hopes, their fears, their judgments of what is worth while.   They may rise to the greatness of an opportunity, seizing its drama, perfecting its art, exploiting its adventure, mastering intellectually and physically the network of relations that constitutes the very being of the epoch.   On the other hand, they may collapse before the perplexities confronting them.   How they act depends partly on their courage, partly on their intellectual grasp.   Philosophy is an attempt to clarify those fundamental beliefs which finally determine the emphasis of attention that lies at the base of character.

Mankind is now in one of its rare moods of shifting its outlook.   The mere compulsion of tradition has lost its force.   It is our business—philosophers, students, and practical men—to re-create and re-enact a vision of the world,

---

[1] " Commuters " in America are season ticket holders who travel daily between city and suburbs, by boat or rail.

including those elements of reverence and order without which society lapses into riot, and penetrated through and through with unflinching rationality. Such a vision is the knowledge which Plato identified with virtue. Epochs for which, within the limits of their development, this vision has been widespread are the epochs unfading in the memory of mankind.